A GRAIN,

A GREEN,

A BEAN

A GRAIN,
A GREEN,
A BEAN

one simple formula,
countless meatless meals

Gena Hamshaw
of *The Full Helping* blog

Photographs by
Ashley McLaughlin

TEN SPEED PRESS
California | New York

Contents

Introduction

Picture this: It's dinnertime. Your fridge is at least semi-stocked with produce. Your pantry contains a few cans of beans and maybe a bag of rice, quinoa, or farro. There's a bookshelf somewhere nearby that's lined with cookbooks, and those cookbooks are littered with Post-it notes flagging the recipes you've been wanting to try. If you were to open your phone, you might find a cooking app or two. You've saved more recipes in Instagram and TikTok than you can count.

In spite of this, and the growling of your stomach as you stare blankly at the kitchen countertop, you have no idea what to cook. Does this sound familiar? If it does, you're not alone.

I've been cooking and writing about food for nearly fifteen years. I have an ample cookbook collection, including a few titles of my own, each filled with recipes I know and love. Like most home cooks nowadays, there's no shortage of accounts I follow on social media for new ideas and inspiration. Even so, I find myself frequently stumped when I ask myself the question: What's for dinner?

For better or for worse, I'm not the only one. Plenty of capable home cooks find themselves in the same scenario, with plenty of recipes at their fingertips and no dinner plan in sight. Given the multitude of cooking resources available to us online and in print, it shouldn't be this hard, right?

Perhaps what's needed isn't another recipe (let alone a giant collection of random recipes) but rather, a formula. This formula can get you thinking strategically about using the ingredients and foods you already have at home to create a meal you're excited to eat. If you're a loyal recipe follower, as I am, then you can use the formula to help you narrow your choices and make selections from the many cookbooks at your disposal.

If you're going to trust in a formula, then it ought to be one that promises good and balanced nutrition as well as a pleasing meal: a quality protein source, energy-sustaining carbohydrates, healthful fats, and plenty of vegetables. If this meal can be relatively complete on its own, sparing you the effort of whipping up a bunch of additional side dishes or accompaniments, so much the better.

Years of feeding myself through times of busyness and times of stillness, periods of culinary inspiration and dreaded food ruts, have helped me to settle on a formula I love and want to share. Ready for it?

A grain, a green, and a bean.

Back to Basics

Grains, greens, and beans. In many ways, these food groups are the building blocks of a plant-based diet. Whole grains, greens, and beans are some of the most nutrient-dense foods on the planet. They've been the foundational ingredients in cuisines for centuries and have sustained communities long before animal protein was always widely available.

Grains, greens, and beans are each rich in vitamins and dietary fiber. Beans are good sources of plant-based protein, as are many grains, especially quinoa and wheat. When these foods are combined, as they are in all the following recipes, they become even more powerfully nourishing.

The notion of grouping grains, greens, and beans together to assemble a meal has existed within the plant-based community for a long time. Educator Matt Frazier, author of *The Plant Based Athlete* and founder of the website No Meat Athlete, popularized the phrase "a grain, a green, and a bean," giving it a handy acronym: AGAGAB. Matt describes AGAGAB as "a simple, one-pot meal that happens to be cheap, filling, and nutritionally outstanding." Combinations of grains, greens, and beans are indeed all those things and more—in a "less is more" kind of way.

Less is more: that call to simplicity hits home for me. Like many vegans, I've gotten accustomed to an ever-widening array of product innovations and restaurant offerings. I love having access to these options, but each time my food bill creeps up I remind myself that they're proverbial icing on the cake.

Some of my favorite plant-based eateries ten and fifteen years ago had sections on their menus devoted to "basics"—always cooked grains, beans, and vegetables—that could be paired with a simple sauce. No matter what other dishes were on the menu, I always found myself drawn to these simple, nourishing meals. With *A Grain, a Green, a Bean*, I'm going back to the basics—for the simplicity, the nutritional value, and the budget-friendly factor!

Part of the beauty of grains and beans is that they're economical as well as satisfying and nutritious. There are exceptions, of course; heirloom and ancient grains are more expensive than conventional counterparts. Foods made with soybeans, such as tempeh, can be more pricy than your average can of chickpeas. For the most part, though, few foods offer more nutrition at a relatively low cost than humble, hearty grains and beans.

The Building Blocks

The categories of "grain," "green," and "bean" might seem self-evident, but there are some nuances worthy of elaboration.

Grains

Grains are the edible seeds of various plants, including oats, rice, corn, and wheat. There's another category of edible seeds called pseudograins, which are harvested similarly to grains and usually grouped with them. Pseudograins are all gluten free, and they include amaranth, buckwheat, and quinoa.

COOKING WHOLE GRAINS

If you're not accustomed to cooking with whole grains, then this book will provide you with a great opportunity to become more comfortable with them. It'll invite you to cook most whole grains the same way you'd cook a pot of pasta: by bringing a big pot of water to a boil, adding the grain, boiling until tender, then draining the grain thoroughly.

Many cooking instructions for grains suggest using a precise ratio of measured cooking water to dry grain. For example, I usually see recipes that suggest a 1:3 ratio of millet to water or a 1:2 ratio of brown rice to water. This can work out perfectly well, but I find it can also be unreliable. Grains might absorb different amounts of liquid depending on how old they are or even which brand of grain you use.

It can be stressful to salvage a pot of bulgur or farro that's dry and burning at the bottom because it wanted more water, or a batch of cooked rice that became soggy from too much liquid. Boiling grains like pasta will give you so much more control over the grain's consistency. I think it's easier, and it results in fluffier, more distinct grains.

There are exceptions. I always cook quinoa with a 1:1¾ ratio of dry quinoa to water, and I use a 1:1½ ratio for most types of white rice. The Oven to Table Recipes section of this book calls for cooking whole grains on a sheet pan or in casserole dishes. In that case, a precise amount of water is specified. Otherwise, you can experience the freedom that comes with boiling grains. You won't have to nervously watch for signs of browning or sticking to the bottom of your cookware!

Grains typically consist of an outer membrane, an inner endosperm, and a core called the "germ" of the grain. When grains are left intact with all these components, then cooked or ground into flour for bread, noodles, or other food products, they're called whole grains.

Refined grains result when the outer membrane of the grain is stripped away from its inner endosperm. White rice, pearled barley, and all-purpose flour are examples of grains that have undergone some amount of refinement.

There's a lot of buzz these days about the value of eating whole grains and grain products, rather than refined grains. There's sound reasoning behind this recommendation: refined grains contain a little less protein, fiber, and vitamins than their whole counterparts. Yet crusty baguettes, bowls of pasta and noodles, and tender flour tortillas are only a few examples of refined-grain foods that are cherished around the world. I value the nutrition of whole grains, but I think foods with refined grains deserve a place in balanced diets, too.

This cookbook presents the "grain" category in a flexible way. Many recipes feature rice, quinoa, wheat berries, millet, and other whole grains. There are also recipes in which the "grain" is a slice of bread, some pasta, or a warm pita pocket. My goal is to help you enjoy grains in as many convenient, enjoyable forms as possible.

Beans (Legumes)

Beans are edible seeds from the Fabaceae, or Leguminosae, family of plants. They're part of a larger category of foods called pulses, which also includes lentils and dried peas. Technically, this book ought to be called *A Grain, a Green, a Legume* because it features dried peas and lentils along with beans.

If any category of food deserves to be called a "superfood," it's beans. While they're usually touted as good sources of plant-based protein, they're also packed with fiber, phytonutrients, and iron.

I knew that beans were good for me as I began to explore plant-based cooking. Having grown up with minimal beans in my diet, however, I didn't know how versatile and fun an ingredient they can be. Beans, lentils, and peas can be mashed, sautéed, simmered, and roasted until crispy. They can be mixed with grains or flour and formed into burgers, patties, and plant-based meatballs. They enrich soups with heartiness and texture, and they're an easy way to make a simple pasta dish higher in protein. I hope the recipes in this book will show you how much potential exists in each can of beans that's sitting in your pantry.

THE MANY FACES OF SOYBEANS

There's one type of bean, the soybean, that's particularly versatile. Many of us are familiar with young soybeans in the form of edamame, but soybeans can also be transformed into a number of other vegan proteins.

Tofu is made with mature soybeans that are soaked, crushed, heated, coagulated, strained into curds, and shaped into blocks. It's a process similar to cheese-making, and the end result is a piece of tofu that can be seared, baked, stir-fried, or crumbled.

Mature soybeans can also be boiled, soaked, drained, shaped into firm cakes, and fermented. This results in tempeh. Because tempeh is made with whole, fermented soybeans, its consistency is more rugged than that of tofu. Instead, tempeh is dense, textured, and hearty. It can be an especially satisfying replacement for animal protein.

Soybeans that have been soaked, stirred, cooked, and dehydrated at low temperatures can become a product called Soy Curls. Manufactured by Butler Foods, soy curls are a wholesome, one-ingredient food that works especially well in any vegan recipe aiming to capture the spirit of a traditional chicken dish (read: tastes like chicken!).

When roasted soybeans are ground into flour, and that flour is defatted and dried, it becomes TVP, or texturized vegetable protein. In its dry form, TVP looks a little bit like bulgur or a coarse couscous. It can be rehydrated in hot liquid to become a chewy, crumbly protein that's especially good for sautéing or using in meaty sauces.

Yuba, also known as tofu (or bean curd) skin, is a protein-rich by-product of the tofu-making process. It's sold in thin, chewy sheets, and it's a great protein for stir-fry meals.

You'll find some additional information about sourcing these soy foods on page 26.

I take the slightly controversial position of almost always using canned beans, rather than dried. For the most part, I don't think canned beans are less flavorful than beans that have been home-cooked from their dried state, and I find them a lot more convenient. They're also every bit as nutritious as beans that have been boiled from dry. Some canned beans are salted, but it's easy to search for low-sodium options, if that's best for you.

If you're in the habit of cooking dried beans or have a monthly bean subscription, it won't be hard to use your scratch-cooked beans in these recipes. My recipes always call for beans in multiples of 1½ cups, which is the amount in a 15-ounce can. For those of you whose pantries are always stocked with a few cans of beans, as mine is, this book will give you a good excuse to continue replenishing your shelves.

One note about the liquid that comes in a can of beans. Many recipes call for draining, rinsing, and then draining these beans again. I think the drained bean canning liquid can be useful sometimes, adding some thickening starch to pastas or helping create ultra-smooth hummus (see page 219). Some recipes in the book specifically call for draining and rinsing beans. But if rinsing isn't specified, you can assume it's fine to merely drain the beans before adding them to the recipe as instructed.

Greens

When you read the word *greens*, your mind might turn immediately to dark leafy greens, such as kale, spinach, bok choy, or Swiss chard. These greens are rightly known for being ultra-nutritious. Originally, it was my thought to make all the "greens" in this book of the dark and leafy variety. As I got into recipe testing, though, I realized the greens I routinely cook with go well beyond those dark leafy greens.

There are many nights when the green component on my plate is broccoli, green bell pepper, green cabbage, brussels sprouts, or green peas. In the spirit of staying true to my own style of cooking, the "greens" in this book include all the above, as well as leeks, green onions, and even copious amounts of herbs. In other words, any vegetable with a green color is fair game.

In allowing yourself to think about greens as a broad, inclusive category, rather than a single group of vegetables, you'll give yourself the flexibility to work with more ingredients. You might also feel comforted to know that the recommendation to "incorporate more greens into your diet"—guidance that dietitians like me dole out all the time—can be met in a realistic, sustainable way.

How to Explore This Book

This book is divided into four main sections: **Bowls & Salads**, **Beans & Greens on Bread**, **Stovetop Meals**, and **Oven to Table Recipes**.

Bowls & Salads may be the types of recipes that come to mind first when you think about cooking with whole grains and beans. These recipes are wholesome, are fresh, and include a lot of texture and color within a single dish.

Beans & Greens on Bread celebrates sandwiches, wraps, toasts, open-faced English muffins, stuffed pita pockets, and toasted tortillas—in other words, any type of recipe in which a bread or wheat product is the central grain.

The **Stovetop Meals** section focuses on one-pot or one-skillet recipes, including pastas, soups and stews, and stir-fries.

Oven to Table Recipes includes casseroles, sheet-pan meals, stuffed vegetables, and other meals that use baking or roasting as the main cooking method.

My hope is that these four sections will demonstrate the many approaches to turning grains, greens, and beans into complete, satisfying meals. The recipes offer a range of preparation times and levels of involvement. Some of the Stovetop Meals and many of the Beans & Greens on Bread are quick and easy, while a few of the grain bowls and baked dishes in the Oven to Table Recipes section are intricate and well suited to cooking in stages. The bottom line is that there's always some combination of grains, greens, and beans to fit your schedule.

Toward the end of the book is a section on **Basics**, which includes sauces, dressings, dips, and other components that find their way into numerous recipes. Taking the time to prepare just one of these multipurpose condiments will set you up for success with the rest of your cooking. For example, Cashew Sour Cream (page 216) appears in no less than 15 recipes in this book! Alternatively, you always have the option to substitute the homemade sour cream, hummus, or guacamole with a store-bought, plant-based alternative.

Finally, I've included five different **Sweet Things**. No, these aren't sweets made with beans and greens. I'm including this tiny chapter because I don't think any experience of food is complete without periodic pauses for something sweet. I'm sharing the five treats that are nearest and dearest to my heart.

As you explore the recipes, I recommend reading each one through from start to finish. That way, you'll be able to spot whether a recipe from the Basics section has been referenced, and you'll know whether there are any preparation steps you should think about in advance of cooking. It's always helpful to have a sense of a recipe's process and timeline before you get to work.

I have food likes and dislikes, as we all do, and the grain, green, and bean categories offer no exception to this rule. I love rice, farro, and quinoa, but I can't stand amaranth (believe me, I've tried). I can eat kale raw or cooked by the pound, but I have a hard time warming up to Swiss chard.

My message to you is this: it's okay to have favorites.

You're allowed to like some whole grains and green vegetables more than others. You don't have to regularly eat every single legume, so long as you try to cook with a few of them. As a dietitian, I can tell you that variety is important, but so is enjoyment and excitement about your food. You don't have to force yourself to eat a type of bean that you don't care for (or can't find) when there are other beans that you love. The same goes for greens and grains.

In the spirit of honoring your preferences and mine, this cookbook favors some of my favorite grains, beans, and greens. There are also opportunities to make substitutions or trades. A few recipes call for kale, collards, spinach, chard, or beet greens—in other words, you can use the dark leafy green that's available and appealing to you.

While I don't always offer or suggest a substitution, know that many of the listed beans can be swapped out for a can of beans that happens to be sitting in your pantry. For instance, I routinely swap cannellini beans for pinto beans, black beans for adzuki beans, and French lentils for brown or green lentils.

If I feel that a particular type of bean is essential to a recipe's success, you can count on me to state that in the recipe headnote. Otherwise, you have an open invitation to make substitutions that feel reasonable to you.

Meal Prep and Storage

I love meal prep. I love it so much that in 2022, I published a cookbook called *The Vegan Week*, which is all about meal prep and the habit of cooking over the weekend—or whenever time allows—so that you start the busy work week with a fridge full of homemade food.

Meal prep is the habit that keeps me cooking, whether I'm motivated to cook or not. There are times when I drag my feet and roll my eyes about having to cook on a Saturday or Sunday, when I'd rather be relaxing. But I'm virtually never sorry to open my fridge after a long workday and find a lovingly prepared, homemade meal.

The recipes in this book aren't as intentionally focused on meal prep as the recipes in *The Vegan Week* are, but most of them lend themselves well to meal prep. I include instructions on storage and freezing at the end of each recipe.

In addition, grains and beans are great components to make in advance. Grains can be cooked, placed in airtight storage containers, and frozen for up to eight weeks. You can make a big batch of grains and freeze the whole thing, or you can portion them out and freeze the portions separately. If you've cooked grains and have a small amount you'd like to tuck away for your future self, move it to the freezer.

The same goes for beans. Once opened, canned beans will typically keep in the fridge for up to four days. If you're making your way through a can slowly, you can extend its life by freezing the last ½ cup or two.

Developing the habit of freezing stored portions of food is so liberating. As a person who lives alone and cooks often, I never worry about having my dishes go to waste. I just transfer them all to the freezer. On weeks when I'm especially busy, it's a bonus to defrost and enjoy nutritious, homemade food with virtually no effort.

To defrost food safely, transfer it to the fridge 24 to 48 hours ahead. This is the slowest yet safest way to defrost. Reheat the food, whether in the microwave, on the stovetop, or in the oven, to a minimum internal temperature of 165°F / 75°C before serving.

Featured Ingredients

Readers often share their concerns with me that vegan diets will be prohibitively expensive or out of reach. I get it: artisanal vegan cheeses, oat-milk lattes, and superfood smoothies don't come cheap, and their availability varies from place to place.

Yet even as inflation drives up the cost of everyday grocery items, there's still good value in a bag of rice, a can of chickpeas, or a pound of lentils. Better still, it's easy to find these ingredients anywhere, whether you shop at a major grocery store or a local co-op. You ought to be able to find most grains, legumes, and vegetables featured in this book at your local grocery. Occasionally, you may need to visit a grocer that specializes in organic and natural foods to find a less popular type of canned bean or particular whole grain. For online shopping, I'm a fan of the Nuts.com website, which has an especially wide selection of whole grains. If you like to cook dried beans from scratch, Nuts.com has a big selection of legumes as well.

While I enjoy vegan specialty products, like vegan cheeses, creamers, or non-dairy butter, I realize their cost may not feel worthwhile to some readers. Having grown accustomed to a food landscape in which there's a commercial vegan stand-in for nearly every animal protein or dairy product, it was a fun challenge for me to formulate these recipes without them.

I was reminded that being vegan is more convenient for me today than it used to be, but the fundamentals of my diet haven't changed much. The foods I rely on now, as a vegan of fifteen years, are similar to the ones I cooked with as I was just starting to explore plant-based foods. You guessed it: most of them are grains, greens, and beans!

It's worth sharing notes on a few ingredients featured in this book.

Adzuki Beans

Adzuki beans, also called red mung beans or aduki beans, have a small shape (they're about the size of navy beans) and a brownish-red color. They can be a little tricky to find in both the dried and canned form, but the Eden Foods brand is often stocked in health food stores and Asian grocery markets. I was introduced to these beans years ago through my interest in macrobiotic cooking, and I love their slightly sweet flavor. If you need a substitution, you can try using navy beans or black beans instead.

Black Rice and Wild Rice

Black rice is the same color as wild rice, but that's where the similarities end. Wild rice isn't actually rice; it's the seed of a semi-aquatic grass and it behaves like rice when it's cooked. Black rice, on the other hand, is a true variety of rice, with a pleasantly chewy texture and slightly nutty flavor. If you look closely, you'll see that its color is almost a deep purple. In fact, black rice also goes by the names purple rice and forbidden rice.

Broth

When broth is called for in one of my recipes, you can assume it's fine to use vegetable broth. However, there are also vegan beef-style and chicken-style broths (or broth concentrates) available, and in some cases, their flavors might be especially well suited for a particular recipe. I call for beef-style or chicken-style vegan broth in the ingredient list if I think one or the other would be best, but vegetable broth is always a fine substitute.

Butter Beans

Butter beans are actually mature lima beans—very unlike the small, green baby limas that are often sold frozen in the United States. Butter beans are what's used to make *gigantes plaki*, a Greek marinated bean dish I grew up with. They're bigger and flatter than most other beans, and they have a wonderfully creamy texture. Several brands, including Goya, Bush's, and Wegmans, make canned butter beans, but you can substitute cannellini beans if you have trouble finding them.

Cashews

Cashews are my culinary MVP, not in their whole form but soaked and blended into cashew cream. Cashew cream is the single best replacement I've tried for heavy cream, milk, and crème fraîche in recipes. Lately, I like to add lemon, lime, and salt to my batches of cashew cream, which makes it reminiscent of sour cream. You'll find this all-purpose condiment in my Basics section (see page 216), and it's referenced in many of this book's recipes. If you need to substitute for it, the recipe offers a specific store-bought vegan substitute.

Farro

Farro is an increasingly easy grain to locate, but it's sold in a few different forms. Pearled farro is farro that has been stripped of its outer coating of bran. It's still rich in fiber and protein, but it cooks in less time than whole farro (about 25 minutes, in comparison to 40 minutes). Pearled farro is the type I purchase most often and recommend for cooking. It's fine to use whole farro in the recipes, but if you do, allow extra cooking time for the grain to become tender. There are also some varieties of par-cooked farro, labeled "quick cooking." Usually, these can be fully cooked with only 10 minutes of boiling. Pearled farro cooks quickly enough to make me happy, but I've used the quick-cooking grain when I am short on time.

Freekeh

Freekeh is a type of young, green wheat that's been roasted or smoked, polished, then cracked. It's similar to bulgur wheat, the grain commonly used in tabbouleh, but with larger pieces and a characteristically smoky flavor. Freekeh can be found in some specialty grocery stores, but a few online storefronts, including Nuts.com, sell it as well. You can substitute bulgur wheat for freekeh in any of my recipes.

Lentils

While I nearly always use canned beans in my cooking, I tend to cook lentils from scratch. This is because there are more lentil varieties available in dried form than canned. Cooking lentils can be a bit of an adventure, in that cooking times vary widely; often this depends on the brand of lentils you use and how old the lentils are. One bag of brown lentils may cook in only 18 minutes, while another might need 30 minutes or more. When cooking lentils, if you think your lentils should be fully cooked, taste a few to be sure. Cooked lentils should be entirely tender, but not mushy or falling apart. If the lentils are still at all hard, give them more cooking time. If they're on the cusp of falling apart, drain them as quickly as you can. Except for red lentils, which cook very quickly and usually benefit from becoming ultra-soft, I recommend cooking lentils as I do grains—in a big pot of boiling water, like pasta, and then draining them before use.

Nutritional Yeast

Nutritional yeast is a form of dried, inactive yeast that can contribute a characteristically cheesy, savory flavor to recipes. It contributes nutrition, too, as it's a great source of B vitamins and a good source of protein.

Nutritional yeast can be purchased online or in natural or organic grocers, either in the bulk section or prepackaged. The Bob's Red Mill, Red Star, and Bragg brands all produce nutritional yeast.

Nutritional yeast is sold either as "flakes" or in a powdered form, both of which are fine for the recipes in this book. The powdered version is harder to find, but I prefer it, as it's easier to stir into pasta dishes or whisk into dressings or sauces. The Frontier Co-op brand makes powdered nutritional yeast that can be ordered online.

Salt

Salt can be a surprisingly divisive and complex ingredient! There are so many different types of salt, and each has a distinctive amount of salinity, or concentration of saltiness.

For this book, I've tried to keep things as simple as possible. When you see "salt" in a recipe's ingredient list, you can assume I'm calling for one of two types of salt: either Morton salt (iodized or not iodized) or fine sea salt. These varieties of salt are relatively easy to find, and they have similar levels of salinity.

If a recipe or step requires a different type of salt, such as Maldon or black salt (kala namak), I list that type specifically in the ingredients.

Soy Curls

Soy curls, described on page 213, are manufactured in the United States by Butler Foods. They can be ordered directly from the company (https://butlerfoods.com/), or you can find a list of retailers by state on the Butler Foods website. Various dehydrated soybean equivalents can be found in Europe, as well.

Soy Sauce, Tamari, Bragg Liquid Aminos, and Coconut Aminos

Soy sauce and tamari are both salty sauces made with fermented soybeans. Tamari typically undergoes longer fermentation than soy sauce, and as a result it has a slightly more complex flavor. Tamari is made with rice, rather than wheat, so it's also safe for gluten-free eaters. Despite these distinctions, you can use soy sauce and tamari interchangeably in my recipes.

Bragg Liquid Aminos is another type of fermented soy sauce, but it has a distinctive, savory flavor. I call for it specifically in some of my recipes, but you can replace it with soy sauce or tamari, if you need to. If you have a soy allergy, coconut aminos is a soy-free sauce with a similar flavor profile. It's much less salty than the three sauces mentioned here, so you may need to increase the amount or add a pinch of salt if you turn to it as a substitute.

Tahini

Tahini is a creamy paste made from ground sesame seeds. It's an ingredient in traditional hummus, but it can be also used to create luxurious, creamy sauces, like the pasta sauce for my gochujang noodles (see page 159). Nearly all tahini sold in major grocery stores is made from roasted, rather than raw, sesame seeds, but if you do happen to find the raw stuff, know that roasted tahini is a better choice for the recipes in this book.

Tempeh

There's some debate about whether it's necessary to steam tempeh, the soy protein described on page 14, prior to cooking it in other ways. Steaming helps reduce some of tempeh's natural bitterness, and it can also make it more absorbent and therefore better for soaking up marinades and sauces. I resisted steaming tempeh for a long time, but over the years I've come to embrace this step as part of preparing a better, more flavorful protein. Some of my recipes call for steaming the tempeh before marinating it, while others call for simmering it in broth before cooking the tempeh in other ways.

Tofu

Most store-bought tofu is labeled as silken or soft, firm, extra firm, or super firm. There's a time and a place for each type, but most of the recipes in this collection call for firm or extra-firm tofu. One exception is the slabs of Eggy Tofu and Sautéed Spinach (page 86) in my Basics section, which I think benefits from the texture of a super-firm variety. Super-firm tofu is also especially rich in protein, so it's sometimes labeled as "high protein" tofu.

Before using any type of firm tofu, press the tofu for 15 minutes to remove some of its moisture. This can be done simply by placing the tofu between two plates, then putting a heavy book on the top plate. Gently drain the water that gets released from the tofu and pat the tofu dry before using it in your recipe.

TVP

TVP (see page 14) is sold by the Bob's Red Mill brand and is easy to find online as well. Many health food stores, especially those that have been around for years, sell TVP in their bulk-bin sections.

Vinegar

I love tart flavors in food, and you'll notice I use many types of vinegars in my dishes. Red and white wine vinegar tend to be easy to find. Balsamic vinegar usually is, too, though it can vary by type and cost. Aged balsamic vinegar, or Balsamic Vinegar of Modena, has a syrupy consistency that makes it great for drizzling and finishing dishes. Less expensive, non-aged balsamic is good in dressings or to add to cooking food.

White balsamic vinegar tastes similarly to red, but it's milder and sweeter. It's subtle enough to stir into a dish without worrying that your meal will become too sweet or too acidic, which is a danger with red balsamic vinegar. White balsamic can be a little hard to find, but many grocery stores carry it. While I know it may seem redundant to have two or three types of balsamic in your kitchen, you'll find that each has a personality of its own and offers a unique contribution to your food.

A grain bowl may be the first recipe that comes to your mind when you think about cooking with whole grains. Call them grain bowls, Buddha bowls, or nourish bowls; usually these are colorful dishes that feature a central cooked grain and an assortment of proteins, vegetables, crunchy components, and sauces.

Salads may be a less obvious vehicle for whole grains, but they're one of my favorite ways to showcase the textures of quinoa, farro, barley, or wheat berries. As an eater who seeks out complete meals, it's rare that I make a salad consisting only of greens or vegetables. Most of my salads are "meal-sized," meaning they consist of a grain, some sort of protein, and healthful fats, as well as vegetables.

Those are the salads you'll find in this section: hearty mixtures that have grains as the starring ingredient. What's the distinction between a grain bowl and a grain salad? I think that's up to you! They're kindred meals, so they belong alongside each other in this chapter.

Grain bowls and complex salads are especially good dishes for meal prep and batch cooking because their multiple components can be made in stages. For example, you can prepare a cooked grain one night and a roasted vegetable another night. You can make a dressing or sauce ahead of time and pop it into the freezer for when you're ready to use it. This way, a little bit of planning can make an otherwise complex bowl easy to assemble.

The bowls and salads in this chapter have a range of complexity. The Lemon Orzo, Tempeh Meatballs, and Roasted Zucchini with Cashew Tzatziki (page 34) is a more time-consuming dish, but if you prepare the meatballs ahead of time, freezing them or storing them in the fridge, the recipe becomes much simpler. On the other hand, Pasta and Three Beans (page 61) is a recipe easy enough to prepare at a moment's notice for a weekend lunch or spontaneous summer get-together.

My third cookbook was called *Power Plates*, but really, it was a book of bowls. In writing that book, I learned how fun and exciting bowls are, and developing the recipes for this section drove that lesson home again. There's inherent simplicity in the idea of putting a few components into a round serving vessel and calling it a meal. Yet there's also the promise of limitless variety. A simple twist—a handful of pickled onions! A new sauce!—makes all the difference. I hope these recipes capture that sense of possibility.

Makes 4 servings

Grain: brown rice
Green: romaine lettuce
Bean: black beans

---

1 cup / 180g long-grain
brown rice

Salt

1 tablespoon freshly
squeezed lime juice

SAUCY BLACK BEANS

1 tablespoon avocado oil

½ red onion, chopped

1½ cups / 240g cooked black
beans, or 1 (15-ounce / 425g)
can black beans, drained
and rinsed

1 teaspoon ground cumin

½ teaspoon smoked paprika

½ teaspoon ground oregano

1 cup / 240ml vegetable broth
or vegan no-chicken broth

1½ tablespoons freshly
squeezed lime juice

Salt

4 cups / 140g tightly packed
chopped romaine lettuce

1 large ripe beefsteak
or heirloom tomato
(or 1½ cups / 240g halved
cherry tomatoes), chopped
into bite-sized pieces

¾ cup / 180ml Cashew
Sour Cream (page 216)

Quick Pickled Onions
(page 208; optional)

BROWN RICE, BLACK BEANS, AND ROMAINE WITH CASHEW SOUR CREAM

I say often that I could live on beans and rice, and this is basically true, but I'm happier when something green (in this case, green and crunchy) is involved. This bowl is an ode to the time-honored, ultra-nutritious combination of beans and rice, which is beloved around the world but often associated with Latin American cuisines. The saucy black beans here are seasoned with cumin, oregano, and smoked paprika—a nod to adobo—and they're great in soft tacos, too. Make the bowls with perfectly ripe, chopped summer tomatoes, even if it means being patient and living in anticipation during the cooler off-season months. When a bowl is this simple, every ingredient deserves to be just right.

Bring a medium pot of water to a boil. Add the brown rice and boil, like pasta, until tender, 35 to 40 minutes. Remove the pot from the heat, then drain the rice and return it to the pot. Cover and allow it to steam for 5 minutes. Uncover the pot and fluff the rice gently with a fork. Season the rice with salt to taste and the lime juice. Re-cover the pot and set aside.

Prepare the black beans. Heat the avocado oil in a medium frying pan over medium heat. Add the red onion and cook, stirring often, for 4 to 5 minutes, until the onion is soft and translucent. Add the beans, cumin, paprika, oregano, broth, and lime juice to the pan. Bring the mixture to a simmer, then reduce the heat to low. Simmer, uncovered, for 7 to 10 minutes, until the beans have thickened considerably. Taste the beans and adjust the salt, spices, and lime juice as desired.

Divide the rice and beans among four bowls. Add one-fourth of the chopped romaine and tomatoes to each bowl. Finish each bowl with a generous spoonful of the Cashew Sour Cream and some pickled onions (if using), and enjoy. The rice, beans, and sour cream will each keep in an airtight container in the fridge for up to 4 days. Add the chopped fresh tomato and romaine just before serving.

BEET COUSCOUS, CHEESY TOFU, GREEN BEANS, AND WATERCRESS

Makes 4 servings

Grain: pearl couscous
Green: green beans
and watercress
Bean: tofu

_____

1 bunch red beets, scrubbed
and trimmed (ideally, 3 or
4 beets each 2 to 3 inches /
5 to 7.5cm in diameter)

⅓ cup / 80ml olive oil, plus
more for roasting the beets

8 ounces / 225g fresh green
beans, trimmed and cut into
2-inch / 5cm pieces

1 cup / 200g pearl couscous

1 batch (3 cups / 550g)
Cheesy Tofu (page 210)

⅓ cup / 80ml white wine
vinegar

2 teaspoons Dijon mustard

1 teaspoon pure maple syrup

1 or 2 garlic cloves, finely
minced or grated

¼ teaspoon fine sea salt

⅛ teaspoon freshly ground
black pepper

¼ cup / 5g finely chopped
fresh dill (optional)

4 cups / 80g lightly packed
baby watercress

There are many things I love about this bowl, but my favorite feature by far is the vibrant pink color that results when roasted beets are folded into plump, chewy pearl couscous. I used to find watercress too spicy, but now I realize that context is everything. The green's sharp, peppery flavor is a perfect foil for the sweetness of roasted beets.

Preheat the oven to 400°F / 200°C.

Rub the beets with a little olive oil, then wrap each beet tightly in aluminum foil. Transfer the wrapped beets to the sheet pan and roast until completely tender when pierced with a knife, 45 to 60 minutes.

Allow the beets to stand at room temperature until cool enough to handle, 15 to 20 minutes. Run the cooled beets under cold running water while you slip off their skins; this should happen easily. Pat the beets dry, then chop them into ¾-inch / 2cm pieces.

While the beets are roasting, bring a large pot of water to a boil. Add the green beans and boil for 5 minutes, until tender but not mushy. Use a strainer to remove the beans from the boiling water and set them aside.

Add the couscous to the pot of hot water. Bring back to a boil and then simmer for 8 to 10 minutes, until the couscous is tender but still chewy. Drain the couscous and transfer it to a large bowl. Add the beets and the Cheesy Tofu.

In a small bowl, whisk together the olive oil, vinegar, mustard, maple syrup, garlic, salt, and pepper. Pour half this mixture over the beets and couscous, reserving the rest. Mix the couscous well, until it's bright pink and the ingredients are evenly incorporated. Fold in the dill (if using).

Divide the beet couscous among four bowls. Divide the watercress and green beans among the bowls as well. Drizzle the green portion of each bowl with the remaining vinaigrette and serve. The beet couscous will keep in an airtight container in the fridge for up to 4 days.

Makes 4 servings

Grain: orzo
Green: zucchini
Bean: tempeh

_____

4 small zucchini, trimmed and quartered lengthwise

1½ tablespoons avocado oil

Salt and freshly ground black pepper

1 cup / 225g orzo

¼ teaspoon garlic powder

1 tablespoon plus 2 teaspoons olive oil

2 teaspoons grated lemon zest

2½ tablespoons freshly squeezed lemon juice

TEMPEH MEATBALLS

1½ cups / 360ml vegetable broth or vegan no-chicken broth

1 (8-ounce / 225g) block tempeh, roughly crumbled

⅓ cup / 35g walnut halves and pieces

½ teaspoon onion powder

½ teaspoon sweet paprika, or ¼ teaspoon smoked paprika

½ teaspoon ground coriander

¾ teaspoon ground cumin

1 teaspoon dried oregano

2 tablespoons nutritional yeast

2 teaspoons soy sauce or tamari

LEMON ORZO, TEMPEH MEATBALLS, AND ROASTED ZUCCHINI WITH CASHEW TZATZIKI

My love of the Gardein brand of vegan meatballs is now a running joke among friends, family, and folks who read my blog. These meatballs were my primary food group during the Covid-19 lockdown. However, I've finally found a homemade meatball that rivals my store-bought favorite. It's made with a simple base of tempeh and walnuts, and it's everything I want plant-based meatballs to be: firm, deeply savory, and nutrient dense. For this recipe, I season the meatballs with cumin and coriander, so they're reminiscent of both the Greek keftede I grew up with and Turkish kofte. I serve them with lemony orzo, some roasted zucchini, and a version of my Cashew Sour Cream that's mixed with a big handful of aromatic, fresh herbs, along similar lines as tzatziki. I'd be lying if I called this recipe quick or easy, but if you prepare it in stages—for example, if you make the meatballs a day or two in advance of everything else—I can almost promise you'll find it worthwhile. It's one of my favorites in this book.

Preheat the oven to 425°F / 220°C. Line a sheet pan with parchment paper or use a nonstick sheet pan.

Place the zucchini spears on the prepared sheet pan. Drizzle the avocado oil over the zucchini, then use your hands to coat the zucchini with the oil. Sprinkle the zucchini lightly with salt and pepper. Place the sheet pan in the oven and roast the zucchini for 10 to 12 minutes, until the bottom sides are browning. Flip the spears and roast for another 8 to 12 minutes, until they're lightly browning on all sides.

Remove the zucchini from the oven, transfer to a plate, and cover loosely with foil or a tea towel. When the sheet pan is cool enough to handle, wash and dry it, and line it with parchment paper (you'll use it for the tempeh meatballs). Reduce the oven heat to 375°F / 190°C.

Bring a medium pot of salted water to a boil. Add the orzo and turn the heat to medium low. Simmer the orzo, uncovered, for 10 minutes, until tender but not mushy. Drain the orzo, run it under cold water, then drain it again thoroughly. Transfer to a medium bowl or storage

CONTINUED

**HERBED CASHEW
SOUR CREAM**

¾ cup / 180ml Cashew
Sour Cream (page 216)

¼ cup / 5g lightly packed
chopped fresh mint

¼ cup / 5g lightly packed
chopped fresh dill

¼ teaspoon garlic powder

Freshly ground black pepper

4 cups / 80g lightly packed
fresh baby spinach

container with a lid. Mix the orzo with ½ teaspoon of salt, the garlic powder, olive oil, lemon zest, and lemon juice. Cover the bowl or container and transfer it to the fridge, keeping the orzo cold while you proceed with the recipe.

Prepare the tempeh meatballs. Fill the same pot with the vegetable broth and bring it to a boil. Reduce the heat to low and add the tempeh. Simmer the tempeh, uncovered, for 10 minutes. Drain the tempeh, reserving 2 tablespoons of the broth.

In a food processor fitted with the S blade, process the walnuts, onion powder, paprika, coriander, cumin, oregano, and nutritional yeast for 15 seconds, until the walnuts and spices are coarsely ground. Add the tempeh, the reserved 2 tablespoons broth, and the soy sauce. Pulse repeatedly until the tempeh and walnuts form a uniform, sticky mixture, about 30 seconds. Remove the blade from the processor and use a spoon to stir everything together well; this will ensure that the mixture is evenly combined. Cover the processor with a tea towel and allow the mixture to rest for 10 minutes.

Use your hands to shape the tempeh mixture into 1-inch / 2.5cm balls; you should have about 16 balls total. Transfer the balls to the prepared sheet pan. Place the sheet pan in the oven and bake the meatballs for 15 minutes. Flip the balls on the sheet and bake for another 5 to 10 minutes, until they're browning.

Prepare the herbed cashew sour cream. In a small bowl, stir the Cashew Sour Cream with the mint, dill, garlic powder, and pepper to taste.

To serve, divide the orzo, spinach, roasted zucchini, and tempeh meatballs among four bowls. Top each portion with one-fourth of the herbed cashew sour cream and enjoy. Alternatively, divide the ingredients into lidded containers and store the herbed cashew sour cream in a separate container. All components will keep in the fridge for up to 4 days.

BASMATI RICE, TOMATO COCONUT LENTILS, AND COLLARD GREENS

Makes 4 servings

Grain: basmati rice
Green: collard greens
Bean: red lentils

_____

The star of this bowl is a batch of creamy coconut red lentils. The lentils are a protein source in the recipe, but because they have a soft texture, they also become a unifying sauce, adding flavors of ginger, garlic, and lime to an otherwise plain mixture of basmati rice and steamed collard greens. An optional power move is to add a scoop of Cashew Sour Cream on top, along with a squeeze of lime juice. If you feel strongly about using brown basmati rice in place of white, that's fine—I've included cooking times for both options.

Place the rice in a medium bowl and add enough cold water to cover it by a few inches. Use your fingers to swish the rice around, rinsing it. The water will turn a little cloudy. Tilt the bowl to pour the water off and repeat this process until the water you add to the rice runs clear—a sign that the rice has released some of its starch, which is the intention. Drain the rice.

Heat ½ tablespoon of the avocado oil in a medium saucepan over medium heat. Add the rice. The wet rice grains will sizzle. Toast the rice grains in the oil, stirring as you go, for 2 to 3 minutes, until the rice smells a little toasty. Pour in the 1½ cups / 360ml water. Bring the water to a boil, then turn the heat to low and cover the rice. Simmer the rice for 12 to 15 minutes, until all the water has been absorbed. (Note: Brown basmati rice will require an additional 10 to 15 minutes of simmering time.)

Remove the pot from the heat and allow the rice to stand for 10 minutes. Fluff the rice, transfer it to a medium bowl or storage container, and cover the bowl while you proceed with the recipe.

Clean the pot, fill it with a few inches of water, and fit it with a steamer attachment. Bring the water to a boil, then add the collard greens to the steamer. Steam the collards for 5 to 10 minutes, until they've reached your desired level of tenderness. Transfer the greens to a bowl or storage container and add some lime juice (if using). Cover the collards while you prepare the lentils.

Drain the water from the pot and return the pot to the stove. Add the remaining tablespoon avocado oil and heat over medium heat.

1 cup / 180g white or brown basmati rice

½ tablespoon and 1 tablespoon avocado oil, divided

1½ cups / 360ml and ¾ cup / 180ml water, divided

1 bunch collard greens, trimmed, thick stems removed, leaves chopped crosswise into 1-inch / 2.5cm-thick ribbons

1½ tablespoons freshly squeezed lime juice, or more as needed

1 small white or yellow onion, chopped

2 garlic cloves, minced

2 teaspoons minced or grated fresh ginger

¼ teaspoon ground coriander

½ teaspoon ground cumin

½ cup / 90g dried red lentils

1 (14½-ounce / 415g) can diced tomatoes, with juices

1 teaspoon salt, or more as needed

½ cup / 120ml full-fat canned coconut milk

Red pepper flakes

Cashew Sour Cream (page 216) and chopped fresh cilantro, green onion tops, or chopped fresh parsley, for serving (optional)

CONTINUED

When the oil is shimmering, add the onion. Sauté the onion, stirring frequently, for 5 minutes, until the onion is soft and translucent. Add the garlic and ginger and cook for another minute, stirring constantly. Add the coriander, cumin, lentils, tomatoes, salt, and the remaining ¾ cup / 180ml water to the pot. Bring the mixture to a simmer, then turn the heat to low and cover the pot. Simmer the lentils for 12 to 15 minutes, until they're tender. Stir the lentils a few times during cooking, as red lentils tend to stick to the bottoms of pots and pans while they cook.

Uncover the lentils and stir in the coconut milk and the 1½ tablespoons lime juice. Season the lentils with the red pepper flakes and additional salt to taste.

Divide the rice, collard greens, and lentils among four bowls. Top each bowl with some lime juice to suit your taste (if desired; I like plenty of it!). Add a scoop of Cashew Sour Cream and some chopped cilantro, green onion tops, or parsley (if using), and serve. Alternatively, transfer the rice, collards, and lentils to individual storage containers. The components will keep in airtight containers in the fridge for up to 4 days.

Makes 4 servings

Grain: pearled barley

Green: cucumber

Bean: tofu

———————

1 cup / 200g pearled barley

12 ounces / 340g ripe Sungold tomatoes, halved

1 seedless cucumber, peeled and chopped

1 batch (3 cups / 550g) Cheesy Tofu (page 210), with marinade

2 tablespoons olive oil

¾ cup / 15g lightly packed thinly sliced fresh basil

Salt and freshly ground black pepper

Freshly squeezed lemon juice, as needed

BARLEY, CHEESY TOFU, AND CUCUMBER
WITH SUNGOLD TOMATOES

Plump, chewy barley is a wonderful choice for grain salads. Barley is generally sold in one of two forms: pearled or hulled. The latter has had only its outer husk removed, while the former has had both husk and bran removed. Pearled barley is a little less nutrient dense than hulled, but I think it has a more pleasant texture; more important, I love that it cooks in about 25 minutes! I use it to make this fresh, summery dish, which bursts with the sweetness of Sungold tomatoes. The marinade for my Cheesy Tofu doubles conveniently as a dressing for the salad. Once you add the tofu to the other ingredients, a couple tablespoons of olive oil are all you need to dress and season the recipe.

Bring a large pot of water to a boil. Add the barley. Boil the barley for 30 minutes, until it's tender yet still has some chew. Drain the barley, then transfer to a large bowl.

Add the tomatoes and cucumber to the bowl. Follow with the Cheesy Tofu and its marinating liquid, then stir in the olive oil and the basil. Mix the ingredients well. Taste and add salt, freshly ground black pepper, and freshly squeezed lemon juice as needed. Serve. The finished salad can be stored in an airtight container in the fridge for up to 3 days.

WHEAT BERRIES, CRISPY CHICKPEAS, AND KALE WITH APPLES

Makes 4 servings

Grain: wheat berries
Green: kale
Bean: chickpeas

_____

If I had to pick a single salad to serve at winter holiday gatherings, it would be this one. Even friends who are convinced they dislike kale seem to enjoy it here. The trick is to dress the kale with a tasty vinaigrette and to "massage" the greens as you work the dressing into them, softening them along the way. Celery and apples add crunch to the salad, as do the Crispy Chickpeas. The salad features a double batch of these beans, so be sure to prepare accordingly! Wheat berries, the grain featured in this recipe, have a longer cooking time than other grains in this book. Soaking them overnight in the fridge will reduce this time a little. If you need to save even more time, you can substitute quicker-cooking pearled barley or farro instead.

Bring a large pot of water to a boil. Add the wheat berries. Boil the wheat berries, like pasta, for 45 to 60 minutes, until they're tender yet hold on to their distinctive chewiness. Drain the wheat berries.

Prepare the vinaigrette. In a medium bowl or liquid measuring cup, whisk together the olive oil, vinegar, mustard, maple syrup, salt, and pepper. When the dressing is emulsified, stir in the shallot and whisk again to combine.

Place the kale in a large bowl. Pour half the dressing (⅓ cup / 80ml) over the greens. Use your hands to "massage" the dressing into the kale, really working the vinaigrette into the greens. After a minute or two, the kale will be reduced in size and more tender. Add the wheat berries, the chickpeas, celery, apple, and cranberries to the bowl, followed by the rest of the dressing. Mix the ingredients well. Taste the salad and adjust salt and pepper as desired. The salad can be stored in an airtight container in the fridge for up to 4 days.

¾ cup / 135g wheat berries

VINAIGRETTE

⅓ cup / 80ml extra-virgin olive oil

3 tablespoons vinegar of choice (champagne, sherry, or white wine)

2 teaspoons Dijon mustard

1 teaspoon pure maple syrup

½ teaspoon fine sea salt

⅛ teaspoon freshly ground black pepper

2 tablespoons finely minced shallot

1 large or 2 small bunches curly kale, stemmed and chopped (about 6 ounces / 180g chopped)

3 cups / 280g Crispy Chickpeas (page 209)

1 cup / 110g diced celery

2 Honeycrisp apples, cored and diced (or other apple variety)

⅓ cup / 40g dried cranberries (or golden raisins)

Makes 4 servings

Grain: spaghetti

Green: lettuce

Bean: red lentils

_____

SPAGHETTI

2 tablespoons olive oil

1 small or ½ large white or yellow onion, diced

4 garlic cloves, minced

1 (28-ounce / 800g) can whole peeled tomatoes, with juices

½ teaspoon cane sugar, agave nectar, or pure maple syrup (optional)

½ cup / 90g dried red lentils

½ teaspoon salt, plus more for seasoning

1 cup / 240ml water

½ cup / 10g tightly packed chopped fresh basil, plus more for garnish

Freshly ground black pepper

12 ounces / 340g spaghetti (or other pasta)

GREEN SALAD

8 cups / 280g Little Gem or baby butter lettuce leaves

2 tablespoons finely snipped fresh chives

3 tablespoons olive oil, or more as needed

1 tablespoon and 1 teaspoon champagne vinegar, or more as needed

1 teaspoon Dijon mustard

¼ teaspoon fine sea salt, or more as needed

Freshly ground black pepper

SPAGHETTI, RED LENTIL POMODORO, AND A GREEN SALAD

If I could have one meal for the rest of my life, I'd choose to eat a big green salad and a bowl of hot spaghetti pomodoro, along with a glass of wine and a slice of chocolate cake for dessert. Pasta with some kind of tomato sauce and a seasonal salad is the meal I order most often in restaurants, and I never get sick of it. When I make this meal at home, I add red lentils to the pomodoro sauce for a boost. The lentils give the dish more texture and more protein, and they make it a little more filling than it would otherwise be. Technically speaking, it's a stretch to call this recipe a bowl, since the green salad is best served on a plate of its own. But the meal reminds me of a bowl, in that it consists of components that would each feel incomplete alone yet are perfect together.

Prepare the spaghetti. Heat the olive oil in a heavy-bottomed medium pot over medium heat. When the oil is shimmering, add the onion. Sauté, stirring frequently, for 10 minutes, until the onion is tender and cooked down. Add the garlic to the pot and cook for 1 minute, until very fragrant, stirring constantly.

Add the tomatoes to the pot. Use a wooden spoon to gently crush the tomatoes. Add the sweetener (if using), lentils, ½ teaspoon salt, and the water to the pot. (The sweetener helps temper the acidity of the tomatoes.) Bring the mixture to a simmer, then turn the heat to low. Cover the pot and simmer for 15 to 20 minutes, until the sauce has thickened and the lentils are tender. Every 5 minutes or so, uncover the pot, give the sauce a stir, and re-cover; red lentils tend to stick to cookware and burn easily, so watch carefully. When the sauce is ready, stir the basil into the sauce. Taste the sauce and add pepper and any additional salt to taste.

While the sauce is cooking, fill a heavy-bottomed large pot with salted water. Bring the water to a boil over medium-high heat. Add the spaghetti and cook according to package instructions, or to your desired texture. Drain the spaghetti.

Prepare the salad. Add the lettuces and chives to a large bowl. In a small bowl, whisk together the oil, vinegar, mustard, and salt. Pour the dressing over the salad greens and toss well. Taste and add pepper and additional salt, oil, or vinegar to your liking.

Divide the cooked spaghetti among four shallow bowls, then top each portion with one-fourth of the sauce and some basil leaves. Serve each bowl with one-fourth of the lettuce salad. The sauce can be stored in an airtight container for up to 5 days in the fridge and frozen for up to 6 weeks. The pasta can be cooked and stored in an airtight container in the fridge for up to 3 days. I recommend making the salad just before serving it.

RICE, EDAMAME, AND SPINACH
WITH STICKY MUSHROOMS

Makes 4 servings

Grain: brown rice
Green: spinach
Bean: edamame

Mushrooms and spinach: I love both vegetables but fear their tendency to become slimy with cooking. Certain preparation methods can prevent this, and I rely on two of them to create these savory bowls. For instance, I cook mushrooms with only a tiny amount of sesame oil in a nonstick pan over relatively high heat—this prevents them from becoming too watery. Then I add them to a salty, sweet, garlicky sauce. Spinach, meanwhile, gets blanched, shocked in an ice bath, squeezed like crazy, and dressed in a tahini and mirin mixture that makes the greens reminiscent of Japanese oshitashi. I know these steps might sound a little fussy, but the textural payoff in the finished dish is worthwhile!

Fill a large bowl with ice cubes and water to make an ice bath. Bring a large pot of water to a boil, then turn the heat to low. Add the spinach, cover, and simmer until the spinach is tender yet still bright green: 45 seconds for regular spinach, 20 seconds for baby spinach. Use a slotted spoon, skimmer, or strainer to remove the spinach from the boiling water and dip into the ice bath. Allow it to cool for 5 minutes, then drain the spinach in a colander.

Add the brown rice to the hot water. Bring the water to a boil and cook the rice, like pasta, for 30 to 35 minutes, until just tender.

Meanwhile, use tea towels or paper towels to press the spinach very firmly to release as much water as possible. Transfer the spinach to a medium bowl.

In a small bowl, whisk together the tahini, mirin, soy sauce, and vinegar. Pour this mixture over the spinach and mix well. Cover the bowl and transfer to the fridge. (The spinach can be prepared and stored in an airtight container in the fridge for up to 1 day before assembling the bowls.)

After the rice has cooked for 30 to 35 minutes, add the edamame to the pot and continue cooking for 4 to 6 minutes, until the edamame is bright green and tender. Drain the rice and edamame, then return them to the pot. Cover the pot and set it aside.

MARINATED SPINACH

12 ounces / 360g chopped fresh spinach leaves and stems, or baby spinach

2 tablespoons tahini

1 tablespoon mirin

1 tablespoon and 1 teaspoon soy sauce

½ tablespoon unseasoned rice vinegar

1 cup / 180g short-grain brown rice

1⅓ cups frozen shelled edamame

STICKY MUSHROOMS

1 teaspoon and 1 tablespoon toasted sesame oil, divided

1 pound / 450g sliced fresh shiitake mushrooms

½ teaspoon cornstarch

2 tablespoons soy sauce

1½ tablespoons unseasoned rice vinegar

1 tablespoon pure maple syrup

4 garlic cloves, minced

2 tablespoons toasted sesame seeds

Chopped green onions, green parts only (optional)

CONTINUED

RICE, EDAMAME, AND SPINACH
WITH STICKY MUSHROOMS, CONTINUED

Prepare the mushrooms. Heat a large, nonstick skillet over medium-high heat. Add the teaspoon of sesame oil, then add the mushrooms. Cook the mushrooms for 8 minutes, stirring often, until they have released their juices and are browning evenly; they should have a chewy texture. Transfer to a plate and return the skillet to the stovetop.

In a small bowl, whisk together the cornstarch, soy sauce, vinegar, and maple syrup. Heat the remaining tablespoon sesame oil over medium-low heat. Add the garlic and sauté, stirring constantly, for 1 minute, until very fragrant. Add the cornstarch mixture to the skillet, followed by the mushrooms. Reduce the heat to low. Cook the mushrooms, stirring constantly, for 2 minutes, until coated with a thick, rich sauce.

To serve, divide the rice and edamame and then the sticky mushrooms among four bowls. Add one-fourth of the cold spinach to the bowls, then top each with ½ tablespoon of sesame seeds. Add some chopped green onions to each bowl (if using), and enjoy. The rice, mushrooms, and spinach can be placed in individual storage containers and stored for up to 3 nights.

BAKED PITA CHIPS, CHICKPEAS, AND SPINACH WITH CURRIED CAULIFLOWER

Makes 4 servings

Grain: pita pockets
Green: spinach
Bean: chickpeas

_____

I'm used to relying on pita bread or pockets as an accompaniment to dips, small salads, and soup. But crispy pita wedges can spruce up a salad the way croutons do. They add crunch and satisfaction, soaking up dressing and softening just a little bit as you eat your way to the bottom of your bowl. Homemade pita chips are fast and easy to make, and it's always rewarding to have a batch on hand. Here, the chips are joined by curried roasted cauliflower florets, chickpeas, and tangy pickled red onions. The bowls can be served right away, or you can prepare the components separately, store them, and enjoy them as part of a meal prep routine. If you do this, be sure to dress the spinach only when you're ready to eat.

Preheat the oven to 400°F / 200°C. Line a sheet pan with parchment paper or aluminum foil, or use a nonstick sheet pan.

Place the cauliflower florets on the prepared sheet pan. Drizzle with the 2 tablespoons avocado oil and mix with your hands to coat the florets. Sprinkle the 1 teaspoon salt, the curry powder, and garlic powder over the florets. Use your hands to mix everything again, rubbing the spices onto the cauliflower until they're evenly coated.

Place the sheet pan in the oven and roast the cauliflower for 15 minutes, then stir the florets on the sheet. Continue to roast for 10 to 15 more minutes, until the cauliflower is tender and browning at the edges. Remove the cauliflower from the oven and allow it to cool. Raise the oven temperature to 425°F / 220°C.

Split the pitas in half crosswise, so that each pocket becomes two flat rounds. Stack the rounds and cut into quarters (for 16 pieces in total). Spread the pita quarters on another sheet pan. Brush the tops of the pita pieces lightly with some of the remaining tablespoon avocado oil. (Alternatively, use avocado oil cooking spray.) Sprinkle the pita wedges with salt and transfer to the oven. Bake for 3 to 5 minutes, until the tops are just browning. Flip the pieces over, and lightly oil and salt the

ROASTED CAULIFLOWER AND PITA

1 large cauliflower, stem trimmed, cut into bite-sized florets and pieces (1½–2 pounds / 680–900g)

2 tablespoons and 1 tablespoon avocado oil, divided

1 teaspoon salt, plus more as needed

2 teaspoons curry powder

½ teaspoon garlic powder

2 whole-wheat pita pockets

3 tablespoons olive oil

1½ tablespoons red wine vinegar

1 teaspoon pure maple syrup

1 small garlic clove, minced

½ teaspoon curry powder

¼ teaspoon ground ginger

6 cups / 140g lightly packed baby spinach

1½ cups / 240g cooked chickpeas, or 1 (15-ounce / 425g) can chickpeas, drained and rinsed

1½ cups / 240g grape or cherry tomatoes, halved

Salt and freshly ground black pepper

½ cup / 65g Quick Pickled Onions (page 208)

CONTINUED

BAKED PITA CHIPS, CHICKPEAS, AND SPINACH
WITH CURRIED CAULIFLOWER, CONTINUED

other sides. Bake for another 3 to 5 minutes, until the pita pieces are crispy and browning on both sides, but not burnt. Remove from the oven and set aside.

Prepare the salad. In a small bowl, whisk together the oil, vinegar, maple syrup, garlic, curry powder, and ginger. Place the spinach, chickpeas, and tomatoes in a large bowl. Pour most of the dressing over, reserving a tablespoon or so for drizzling onto the assembled bowls. Mix well and season as desired with additional salt and pepper.

Divide the salad mixture among four bowls. Top each bowl with one-fourth each of the cauliflower and crispy pita chips, followed by 2 heaping tablespoons each of the pickled onions. Drizzle the last of the vinaigrette over the bowls and enjoy. The roasted cauliflower and pita pieces can be stored in airtight containers in the fridge for up to 4 days. The chips can be re-crisped by warming on a sheet pan in a 350°F / 175°C oven for 10 minutes. Store the vinaigrette separately and dress the portions of spinach, chickpeas, and tomatoes right before serving.

QUINOA, CRUMBLED CHEESY TOFU, ROASTED CORN, AND ROMAINE

Makes 4 servings

Grain: quinoa
Green: romaine lettuce
Bean: tofu

_____

This hearty salad is loosely inspired by *elote*, the grilled street corn that's served with a tangy, creamy sauce. As a small-apartment dweller in New York City, I don't have access to a grill, so I roast corn kernels in my oven instead. Oven roasting imparts some of the same sweet, smoky flavor as grilling, and it gives me the option to use frozen kernels in wintertime, when fresh corn isn't available to me. Likewise, you have the option to use either fresh or frozen corn in this recipe.

Preheat the oven to 425°F / 220°C. Line a sheet pan with aluminum foil or use a nonstick sheet pan.

Spread the corn kernels on the prepared sheet pan. Drizzle the kernels with the avocado oil and a generous pinch of salt, and stir the kernels on the sheet to coat well. Roast for 15 minutes and stir again. Roast the kernels for an additional 10 to 15 minutes, until they're golden brown. Remove the corn from the oven and allow it to cool for 15 minutes.

While the corn roasts, rinse the quinoa in a fine-mesh strainer. Add the quinoa to a medium pot along with the water. Bring the water to a boil, cover, and turn the heat to low. Simmer for 13 minutes, then remove the pot from the heat. Allow the quinoa to stand for 5 minutes, then fluff it with a fork. Re-cover and allow the quinoa to cool for 15 to 30 minutes (the quinoa shouldn't be piping hot when you mix it with the chopped romaine).

Add the corn and quinoa to a large bowl. Add the Cheesy Tofu, along with its marinade. Stir well, then add the romaine, red onion, red pepper, and cilantro to the bowl.

Prepare the dressing. In a small bowl, whisk together the Cashew Sour Cream, lime juice, olive oil, agave nectar, chili powder, paprika, and cayenne (if using). Pour this dressing over the salad and mix well. Taste the salad and add additional salt, if desired, and enjoy. The roasted corn, quinoa, and Cheesy Tofu can be stored in individual airtight containers for up to 3 days in the fridge. Mix the components with the dressing and the rest of the salad ingredients directly before serving. Once tossed together, the salad can keep overnight in the fridge.

3 heaping cups / 455g fresh or frozen corn kernels, or fresh kernels cut from 4 large or 6 small ears of corn

1 tablespoon avocado oil

Salt

1 cup / 180g white quinoa

1¾ cups / 415ml water

1 recipe Cheesy Tofu (page 210), crumbled, with marinade

3 cups / 120g packed shredded romaine lettuce

⅓ cup / 45g finely diced red onion

⅔ cup / 100g seeded and diced red bell pepper, or ½ cup / 100g diced roasted red bell pepper

¼ cup / 10g chopped fresh cilantro

DRESSING

½ cup / 120ml Cashew Sour Cream (page 216) or store-bought vegan sour cream or mayonnaise

1 tablespoon freshly squeezed lime juice

1 tablespoon olive oil

1 teaspoon agave nectar or pure maple syrup

¾ teaspoon chili powder

¼ teaspoon smoked paprika

Small pinch cayenne (optional)

Makes 4 servings

Grain: black rice
Green: broccoli
Bean: tempeh

_____

8 ounces / 225g tempeh, cut into 1-inch / 2.5cm cubes

1 cup / 180g black rice

3 broccoli crowns, cut into florets and stem pieces

1½ tablespoons and ½ cup / 120ml avocado oil, divided

3 tablespoons / 30g and 1 teaspoon finely minced or grated fresh ginger, divided

1 bunch green onions (about 7 / 70g), green and white parts, finely chopped crosswise

½ teaspoon salt

2 teaspoons toasted sesame oil

2 tablespoons tamari

1 tablespoon unseasoned rice vinegar

1 teaspoon pure maple syrup

2 garlic cloves, finely minced or grated

Pinch red pepper flakes

BLACK RICE, TEMPEH, AND BROCCOLI
WITH GINGER SCALLION OIL

Of many recipes I've made in the past, I've said, "This recipe is all about the sauce." But this one really is all about the sauce! The star of the show here is ginger scallion oil. To make it, you simply pour piping-hot oil over a mixture of grated ginger, finely chopped green onions, and salt. The sauce can elevate just about anything you add it to, including these simple bowls of crispy broccoli, gingery tempeh, and black rice. Double the sauce, if you like, and reserve the extra for noodles, rice, tofu, cooked greens, roasted vegetables, or dumplings. (The sauce will keep in an airtight container in the fridge for up to 2 weeks, though my supply never lasts that long.)

Preheat the oven to 425°F / 220°C. Line a sheet pan with parchment paper or use a nonstick sheet pan.

Fill a medium pot with a few inches of water and bring the water to a boil. Fit the pot with a steamer attachment. Add the tempeh to the steamer and steam for 10 minutes, then set the tempeh aside.

Remove the steamer attachment and add enough additional water to fill the pot. Bring the water to a boil. Add the rice and boil, like pasta, for 30 minutes, until the grains are tender. Drain the rice through a fine-mesh strainer, then return the rice to the pot. Cover the rice until you're ready to serve it.

Place the broccoli on the prepared sheet pan in a single layer. Drizzle with 1½ tablespoons of the avocado oil, then mix the florets and oil together. Transfer the sheet to the oven and roast the broccoli for 12 minutes, until the bottoms of the florets are browning. Flip the pieces and roast for another 5 to 8 minutes, until crispy and browning throughout.

In a small bowl, combine 3 tablespoons / 30g of the ginger, the green onions, and salt. Add the remaining ½ cup / 120ml avocado oil to a medium frying pan. Heat the oil for 3 to 4 minutes over medium-high heat, until gently bubbling. Drop a piece of green onion into the oil to test its readiness; it should sizzle aggressively when added. When the oil is hot enough, pour it over the green onion mixture in the bowl. Stir the mixture well, cover the bowl, and set aside.

CONTINUED

Add the sesame oil to the frying pan over medium heat. Add the tempeh cubes and sauté for about 4 minutes, flipping the cubes periodically so all sides are just starting to turn golden.

In a small bowl, whisk together the tamari, vinegar, maple syrup, garlic, red pepper flakes, and the remaining teaspoon ginger, then add this mixture to the hot pan with the tempeh. Continue cooking the tempeh for 2 to 3 minutes, until the sauce has been absorbed and the tempeh is crisping and darkening.

Divide the rice, broccoli, and tempeh among four bowls. Spoon a generous amount of the ginger scallion oil over each bowl, then mix well. The rice, tempeh, and broccoli will keep in individual airtight containers in the fridge for up to 4 days, and the ginger scallion oil will keep for up to 2 weeks.

PASTA, TEMPEH RATATOUILLE, AND ARUGULA

Makes 4 servings

Grain: pasta
Green: arugula
Bean: tempeh

I love ratatouille, and I love it even more when it cooks self-sufficiently on a sheet pan. Here, I make oven-roasted ratatouille heartier with the addition of seasoned tempeh cubes. You can serve the mixture over toast or a whole grain, in which case it could be part of the Beans & Greens on Bread section. I especially like to eat it with pasta, lemony arugula, and a generous drizzle of balsamic vinegar. This recipe calls for not one but two types of balsamic vinegar: white balsamic for seasoning the ratatouille and the Balsamic Vinegar of Modena (or another syrupy variety) for drizzling. If you're not the balsamic enthusiast I am and don't have both types at home, it's no problem. You can use whatever type of balsamic vinegar you do have for both purposes.

Preheat the oven to 400°F / 200°C.

Spread the eggplant, zucchini, red pepper, onion, tomatoes, and garlic cloves on a sheet pan. Drizzle the vegetables with the avocado oil. Use your hands to mix the oil and vegetables well. Sprinkle the vegetables very generously with salt and pepper. Cover the sheet pan tightly with a layer of foil, then place it on the top rack of the oven. Roast for 30 minutes. Remove the foil from the sheet pan and stir the vegetables. Place the sheet pan back in the oven and roast, uncovered, for 15 more minutes. Stir the vegetables again and roast for 15 to 25 more minutes, until the mixture is very saucy and the eggplant is meltingly tender. Stir in the white balsamic vinegar. Taste the ratatouille and adjust the salt, pepper, and vinegar as desired.

While the ratatouille roasts, line another sheet pan with parchment paper or aluminum foil or use a nonstick sheet pan. In a large, heavy-bottomed pot, bring the broth to a boil over high heat, then turn the heat to low. Add the tempeh cubes. Simmer, uncovered, for 10 minutes, until the tempeh has absorbed a significant portion of the broth. Drain the tempeh, then transfer it to the sheet pan. In the last 20 minutes of cooking the ratatouille, add the tempeh to the lower rack of the oven.

1 small globe eggplant, trimmed and cut into 1-inch / 2.5cm cubes

1 zucchini, trimmed and cut into 1-inch / 2.5cm cubes

1 large red bell pepper, seeded and cut into 1-inch / 2.5cm pieces

1 red onion, roughly chopped

1 pound / 450g grape or cherry tomatoes

6 garlic cloves

2 tablespoons avocado oil

Kosher salt and freshly ground black pepper

1 tablespoon white balsamic vinegar, plus more as needed

2 cups / 480ml vegetable broth

1 (8-ounce / 225g) block tempeh, cut into 1-inch / 2.5cm cubes

8 ounces / 225g pasta, any medium shape

4 cups / 80g lightly packed baby arugula

Syrupy balsamic vinegar (such as Aceto Balsamico di Modena IGP), for serving

CONTINUED

PASTA, TEMPEH RATATOUILLE, AND ARUGULA,
CONTINUED

Bake for 10 minutes, then use tongs to flip the cubes over and bake for another 10 minutes, until all sides of the tempeh are starting to brown.

Add the baked tempeh cubes to the finished ratatouille and mix well.

Rinse the large pot, then fill it with salted water. Bring to a boil over high heat. Add the pasta and cook to your desired texture, or according to package instructions. Drain the pasta.

Divide the pasta and tempeh ratatouille among four bowls. Add a lightly packed cup of arugula to each bowl, then drizzle the bowls generously with the syrupy balsamic. Mix and serve. The tempeh ratatouille and pasta can be stored in individual airtight containers in the fridge for up to 5 days. Add the fresh arugula directly before enjoying.

PASTA AND THREE BEANS

Makes 4 servings

Grain: rotini, fusilli, or penne
Green: green beans
Bean: kidney beans, chickpeas

───────────

This easygoing dish is a combination of two of my favorite summertime lunches: classic three-bean salad and pasta salad. Instead of adding diced red or white onion, as is traditional in a three-bean salad, I use a generous amount of Quick Pickled Onions. The pickled onions, combined with lots of chopped fresh herbs, add character to an otherwise simple recipe.

Fill a heavy-bottomed large pot with a few inches of water and add a steamer insert. Bring the water to a boil. Add the green beans and steam for 5 to 6 minutes, until the beans are tender but not mushy. Allow the beans to cool until they can be handled, then cut them crosswise into 1½-inch / 4cm pieces.

Discard the steaming water. Fill the pot with fresh water and add about 1½ teaspoons salt. Bring the water to a boil, then add the pasta. Cook the pasta according to package instructions, or to your preferred texture. Drain the pasta, run it under cold water for about 1 minute, then drain it again. Use a tea towel to pat the pasta dry a bit.

In a very large bowl, combine the cannellini beans, chickpeas, celery, pickled onions, parsley, and dill. Add the pasta and green beans.

In a small bowl or liquid measuring cup, whisk together the olive oil, vinegars, maple syrup, mustard, and about ¼ teaspoon salt. Pour this dressing over the salad ingredients and mix well. Taste and add additional vinegar or salt and pepper to your liking. Serve the salad. The salad can be stored in an airtight container in the fridge for up to 4 days.

12 ounces / 340g fresh green beans, trimmed

Salt

8 ounces / 225g medium pasta (such as rotini, fusilli, or penne)

1½ cups / 280g cooked kidney or cannellini beans, or 1 (14.5-ounce / 415g) can kidney or cannellini beans, drained and rinsed

1½ cups / 240g cooked chickpeas, or 1 (15-ounce / 425g) can chickpeas, drained and rinsed

½ cup / 55g finely diced celery

⅔ cup / 85g Quick Pickled Onions (page 208), drained

¼ cup / 10g chopped fresh parsley

½ cup / 5g chopped fresh dill

¼ cup / 60ml olive oil

2½ tablespoons white wine vinegar or red wine vinegar, or more as needed

1 tablespoon apple cider vinegar

1 teaspoon pure maple syrup or agave nectar

1½ teaspoons Dijon mustard

Freshly ground black pepper

Makes 4 servings

Grain: freekeh
Green: arugula
Bean: chickpeas

———————

1½ cups / 240g
cooked chickpeas, or
1 (15-ounce/425g) can
chickpeas, drained and rinsed

½ cup / 70g diced red onion

¼ cup / 30g chickpea flour

1 teaspoon salt

½ teaspoon ground cumin

1 garlic clove, minced

½ cup / 10g tightly packed
fresh parsley

½ cup / 10g tightly packed
fresh cilantro

1 tablespoon olive oil

1 cup / 160g freekeh

4 cups / 80g packed baby
arugula

Quick Pickled Onions
(page 208) and chopped
tomato or cucumber, for
serving (optional)

Tahini Sauce (page 214),
for serving

FREEKEH, HERBED CHICKPEA CAKES, AND ARUGULA

Freekeh is a type of wheat, like bulgur or farro. What's distinctive about freekeh is its smoky flavor, which develops when young stalks are roasted, then rubbed, releasing the toasted grains inside. Freekeh can be tricky to locate (see page 25 for more on sourcing), but its unique taste makes it a grain well worth finding and cooking with! In this dish, a bed of freekeh is topped with herbaceous chickpea cakes, which are reminiscent of falafel, a tangy tahini sauce, and some peppery arugula. The chickpea cakes are a great plant protein to meal-prep, so it's worthwhile to make a double batch and freeze some for future use.

Preheat the oven to 375°F / 190°C. Line a sheet pan with parchment paper or use a nonstick sheet pan.

In a food processor fitted with the S blade, place the chickpeas, red onion, chickpea flour, salt, cumin, garlic, parsley, cilantro, and olive oil. Pulse repeatedly a few times, then process for 20 to 30 seconds. You're aiming for a mixture with flecks of herbs throughout, but not a uniform puree; some small pieces of chickpea are okay. Use your hands to shape this mixture into cakes about 1½ inches / 4cm in diameter and ½ inch / 3cm thick (you should get about 12 total). The mixture will be a little wet and sticky, so be patient as you work.

Transfer the cakes to the prepared sheet pan and bake for 15 minutes. Use a spatula to gently flip the cakes over, then bake for another 10 to 12 minutes, until both sides are golden brown. Remove from the oven and set aside.

While the chickpea cakes cook, bring a medium pot of water to a boil. Add the freekeh and boil, uncovered, for 20 minutes, until the grains are tender but retain some chewiness. Drain the freekeh thoroughly, return it to the pot, and fluff it with a fork.

Divide the freekeh, chickpea cakes, and arugula among four bowls. Add any additional accompaniments you like, then drizzle the bowls generously with the tahini sauce and serve. The cakes and cooked freekeh will keep in separate airtight containers for up to 4 days in the fridge or 6 weeks in the freezer.

COLD KIMCHI NOODLES, EGGY TOFU, AND CUCUMBER

Makes 4 servings

Grain: somen noodles
Green: cucumbers
Bean: tofu

I've made numerous noodle dishes that incorporate kimchi, but the noodles in this bowl recipe are my favorite. They were inspired by Sue, the talented creator behind the My Korean Kitchen blog. Sue introduced me to kimchi bibim-guksu, a Korean cold noodle dish that incorporates chopped kimchi and kimchi brine, as well as a spicy gochujang and vinegar marinade. I like to dress somen noodles with this marinade, then serve the kimchi alongside or on top of them. Keeping the kimchi separate, rather than folding it into the noodles, helps me better appreciate the texture of both components—delicate noodles and chewy cabbage. The green here, chopped cucumbers, is simple, and the bean is an Eggy Tofu square. I love to top the bowls with a drizzle of gochujang-spiked vegan mayonnaise, but that's just a starting point: toasted sesame seeds, chopped green onions, red pepper flakes or chili crisp, and hot sauce all work to enhance the meal.

Bring a medium pot of water to a boil and add the somen noodles. Boil for 2 minutes, then drain the noodles and rinse for about 1 minute under cold running water. Drain the noodles again.

In a medium bowl, place the sesame and avocado oils, gochujang, rice vinegar, and maple syrup and whisk until smooth. Add the noodles and gently mix them into the sauce, until all the noodles are a light orange color. The noodles can be prepared up to 3 days in advance of making the bowls.

Divide the noodles among four bowls or individual storage containers, if meal-prepping. Add ½ cup of kimchi and one-fourth of the cucumber to each bowl. Top the bowls with the Eggy Tofu.

In a small bowl or liquid measuring cup, whisk the mayonnaise, gochujang, and vinegar together. Drizzle this over the bowls and serve or store the dressing in small containers if meal-prepping. Top with any additional accompaniment you like and enjoy.

COLD NOODLES

8 ounces / 225g somen noodles (or udon or soba noodles)

1 tablespoon toasted sesame oil

1 tablespoon avocado oil

1½ tablespoons gochujang

1½ tablespoons unseasoned rice vinegar

2 teaspoons pure maple syrup

2 cups vegan kimchi of choice

1 large seedless cucumber, peeled or unpeeled, quartered lengthwise and chopped

1 square Eggy Tofu (page 212), or 1 store-bought vegan egg (such as Just Egg Folded or Crafty Counter Wunder Egg)

⅓ cup / 75g vegan mayonnaise (such as Vegenaise) or Cashew Sour Cream (page 216)

1½ tablespoons gochujang

2 tablespoons unseasoned rice vinegar

Sliced green onions, green parts only; toasted sesame seeds; or crushed red pepper flakes, for topping (optional)

MISO SOY NOODLES, EDAMAME, AND CUCUMBERS

Makes 4 servings

Grain: udon noodles
Green: cucumber
Bean: edamame

_____

This bowl came together when I had plans to host a friend for dinner on an especially hot summer day. Even with the AC on, I couldn't fathom roasting or sautéing a thing. Instead, I whipped up these savory miso soy noodles and topped them simply, with marinated cucumbers and steamed edamame. We were both happy, and the miso soy sauce has become a personal favorite. Whisked tahini and avocado oil help to give it an unctuousness that's reminiscent of miso butter.

Slice the cucumbers crosswise into ⅛-inch / 3mm slices. In a medium bowl, whisk together the 2 tablespoons rice vinegar, the cane sugar, sesame oil, salt, and garlic powder. Add the cucumbers and mix well. Cover the bowl and transfer to the fridge.

In a medium pot fitted with a steamer attachment, bring a few inches of water to a boil over high heat. Add the edamame and steam for 5 minutes, until the beans are bright green and tender.

Set the edamame aside and fill the pot with fresh water. Bring the water to a boil over high heat. Add the udon noodles and cook according to package instructions, about 6 minutes. Drain and rinse the noodles under cold running water. Spread a tea towel on a sheet pan and lay the drained noodles on top to drain a little more.

Prepare the miso soy sauce. In a small bowl or liquid measuring cup, whisk together the miso, tahini, and avocado oil. When the mixture is smooth, whisk in the soy sauce and rice vinegar.

Place the udon noodles in a medium bowl, add the miso sauce, and mix well. Divide the noodles among four bowls. Top each bowl with one-fourth of the cucumbers, the edamame, and the cubed avocado. Drizzle each bowl with a bit of the extra liquid from the cold cucumbers. Top each bowl with 1 teaspoon of the sesame seeds and 1 tablespoon of the green onions (if using). Crumble a nori sheet (if using) over each bowl and enjoy. The noodles, cucumbers, and shelled edamame can be stored in individual airtight containers in the fridge for up to 3 days. Assemble the bowls when ready.

4 mini seedless cucumbers, ends trimmed

2 tablespoons unseasoned rice vinegar

1 teaspoon cane sugar

1 teaspoon toasted sesame oil

¼ teaspoon fine salt

⅛ teaspoon garlic powder

1½ cups / 225g frozen shelled edamame

8 ounces / 225g udon noodles

MISO SOY SAUCE

1 tablespoon white miso

2 tablespoons tahini

1 tablespoon avocado oil

1 tablespoon soy sauce or tamari

2 tablespoons unseasoned rice vinegar

1 large Hass avocado, pitted and cut into small cubes

4 teaspoons toasted white or black sesame seeds

¼ cup / 20g chopped green onion, green parts only (optional)

4 roasted, salted nori sheets (optional)

Makes 4 servings

Grain: farro

Green: kale, green beans

Bean: black lentils

————————

1 large bunch Tuscan kale, thick stems trimmed, leaves chopped crosswise into ¾-inch / 2cm pieces

12 ounces / 340g fresh green beans, trimmed

1 cup / 180g pearled farro

½ cup / 90g black or French lentils

3 tablespoons olive oil

1½ tablespoons freshly squeezed lemon juice

¾ tablespoon white wine vinegar or champagne vinegar

1 teaspoon Dijon mustard

¼ teaspoon salt, or more as needed

¾ cup / 100g packed Quick Pickled Onions (page 208)

1 large Hass avocado, pitted and chopped

2 tablespoons snipped fresh chives (optional)

Freshly ground black pepper

FARRO, LENTILS, AND KALE WITH AVOCADO AND GREEN BEANS

Candle, a vegan restaurant in New York City with previous incarnations as Candle Cafe and Candle 79, serves a hearty salad that features grilled Tuscan kale. I love this salad, and over the years I've worked on perfecting a homemade version. Since I don't have a grill, I boil the kale and let the cooked greens cool in the fridge while I make the farro and lentils that are this recipe's whole grain and legume, respectively. All three central ingredients—kale, farro, and lentils—should be patted dry with tea towels before being mixed and dressed. If any component is overly wet when you add the dressing, you'll end up with a soggy and diluted salad—not ideal! If you use pearled farro, which is my recommendation, it requires the same amount of cooking time as the lentils, so you can boil them conveniently together in a single pot.

Fill a large pot halfway with water and bring to a boil over high heat. Add the kale and boil for 2 minutes, until the kale has wilted, then add the green beans. Continue boiling the vegetables for 3 more minutes, until tender yet still bright green and with some firmness. Drain the vegetables. Spread a tea towel on a large sheet pan and add the vegetables. Top with another tea towel and pat the vegetables dry. Transfer the vegetables to a bowl or storage container, cover, and keep in the fridge while you proceed with the recipe.

Fill the pot with fresh water and bring to a boil over high heat again. Add the farro and lentils. Boil for 30 to 35 minutes, until both farro and lentils are tender but not mushy. Drain the farro and lentils thoroughly, then repeat the drying process used for the kale and green beans.

In a small bowl, whisk together the oil, lemon juice, vinegar, mustard, and salt.

In a large bowl, combine the kale and beans, farro and lentils, the pickled onions, avocado, and chives (if using). Pour the dressing over them. Mix well, until the avocado is coating everything nicely. Taste and add salt and pepper as needed. Serve immediately. The dressed salad can be stored in an airtight container in the fridge for up to 3 days.

ORZO, CHICKPEAS, AND ROASTED CARROTS WITH SUGAR SNAP PEAS AND DILL

Makes 4 servings

Grain: orzo
Green: sugar snap peas, dill
Bean: chickpeas

_____

1 pound / 450g carrots, trimmed, peeled, halved lengthwise, and cut into 1-inch / 2.5cm pieces

1 tablespoon avocado oil

Salt

1 cup / 225g orzo

6 ounces / 180g fresh sugar snap peas, halved crosswise

1½ cups / 240g cooked chickpeas, or 1 (15-ounce / 425g) can chickpeas, drained and rinsed

¼ cup / 10g chopped fresh dill

½ cup / 40g thinly sliced green onions, both green and white parts

2 tablespoons olive oil, or more as needed

1 tablespoon red or white wine vinegar, or more as needed

Freshly ground black pepper

I have such a soft spot for orzo, the tiny pasta I grew up eating as the daughter of a first-generation Greek-American mom. Thanks to my heritage, I'm also a huge fan of dill, and in this recipe, those two ingredients come together in a colorful salad for late spring or early summer. The roasted carrots give the salad substance, while the crispy sugar snap peas and herbs keep it fresh and bright. If you have a batch of Quick Pickled Onions (page 208) in the fridge, you can add yet another element to the salad by tossing them in at the last moment.

Preheat the oven to 400°F / 200°C. Line a sheet pan with parchment paper or aluminum foil or use a nonstick sheet pan.

Spread the carrots on the prepared sheet pan and drizzle with the avocado oil. Mix well so carrots are evenly coated with oil. Spread the carrots in an even layer and sprinkle lightly with salt. Roast for 30 minutes, until they're tender and lightly browning, stirring once halfway through baking.

While the carrots roast, bring a large, heavy-bottomed pot of salted water to a boil over high heat. Add the orzo and boil for 8 to 10 minutes, until the orzo is tender yet still has some pleasant chewiness. In the last 3 minutes of boiling, add the sugar snap peas to the pot. Drain the orzo and peas well and transfer to a large bowl. Add the roasted carrots, the chickpeas, dill, and green onions to the bowl.

In a small bowl, whisk together the olive oil, vinegar, and ½ teaspoon of salt. Pour this mixture over the salad and toss the ingredients, mixing well. Taste the salad; adjust the oil, vinegar, and salt to your liking and add pepper as desired. Serve. The salad can be stored in an airtight container in the fridge for up to 3 days.

Makes 4 servings

Grain: red quinoa
Green: arugula
Bean: chickpeas

_____

1 cup / 180g red or white quinoa

1¾ cups / 415ml water

6 cups / 120g lightly packed fresh baby arugula

1 cup / 160g cherry or grape tomatoes, halved

1½ cups / 140g Crispy Chickpeas (page 209)

1½ tablespoons olive oil

1 tablespoon freshly squeezed lemon juice

Salt and freshly ground black pepper

1⅓ cups / 320g Chickpea Hummus (page 219)

RED QUINOA, HUMMUS, AND ARUGULA WITH CRISPY CHICKPEAS

This salad features chickpeas two ways: pureed in the form of hummus, and roasted whole until crispy. The hummus is layered in the bottom of each serving dish, which is an idea that I got from a local Mediterranean restaurant. The dish comprised crisp greens, tomato, and cooked quinoa on a bed of creamy hummus. I could see that the intention was for me to mash the ingredients together, so that the hummus would become both a component of the meal and part of the salad's dressing. How had I never thought to do this before? Now I do—and this recipe is my favorite example. Hummus creates a bed for the other ingredients. When you mix it all up, you'll find great textural complexity in the creamy bean spread, fluffy quinoa, and crispy, whole roasted chickpeas.

Place the quinoa in a fine-mesh strainer and rinse under cold running water for about 30 seconds. Transfer the quinoa to a medium pot and add the water. Bring to a boil over medium-high heat. Cover the pot, turn the heat to low, and simmer until all the water has been absorbed, about 13 minutes. Remove the pot from the heat and allow it to sit for 5 minutes. Uncover the pot and fluff the quinoa gently with a fork. Re-cover the pot and set aside.

In a large bowl, toss together the arugula, tomatoes, Crispy Chickpeas, olive oil, and lemon juice. Taste the greens and add salt and pepper as desired. The greens should be lightly dressed, as the hummus will also become part of their dressing.

Spread ⅓ cup / 80ml of hummus in the bottoms of four serving bowls. Add one-fourth of the greens and chickpea mixture to each bowl, followed by one-fourth of the quinoa. Mix the ingredients as you eat, blending the hummus with the other components. The cooked quinoa, hummus, and chickpeas will keep for up to 4 days in separate airtight containers in the fridge. Then, dress the arugula, tomatoes, and chickpeas right before serving.

Makes 4 servings

Grain: brown rice

Green: kale

Bean: tofu

———————

1 cup / 180g short- or long-grain brown rice

MARINATED KALE

1 large bunch curly kale, stemmed, leaves chopped (about 6 ounces / 170g)

3 tablespoons olive oil

1½ tablespoons apple cider vinegar

1 teaspoon Dijon mustard

¼ teaspoon garlic powder, or 1 garlic clove, minced

½ teaspoon pure maple syrup

¼ teaspoon fine sea salt

1 tablespoon avocado oil

1 small or ½ large white or yellow onion, chopped

1 bell pepper (any color), cored, seeded, and chopped

8 ounces / 225g fresh button mushrooms, cleaned and sliced

2 tablespoons tahini

2 tablespoons water

½ tablespoon freshly squeezed lemon juice

1 teaspoon Dijon mustard

1 tablespoon Bragg Liquid Aminos or soy sauce

1 (14-ounce / 400g) block extra-firm or firm tofu, pressed (see page 212)

2 tablespoons nutritional yeast

BROWN RICE, SCRAMBLED TOFU, AND MARINATED KALE

In my first year as a vegan, I probably cooked tofu scramble more than any other food. To make a tofu scramble, you crumble a block of extra-firm tofu into small pieces, season it with turmeric, which turns it a pale yellow, and scramble it in a hot pan, just as you'd scramble eggs. The tofu can be served for breakfast or brunch, but as a fledgling home cook I made many dinners of it. Tofu scramble is still a mainstay for me at any time of day; it's a nutritious, easygoing meal that can accommodate whatever vegetable mix-ins you have in the fridge. My favorite way to plate my tofu scramble is with warm rice and a marinated kale salad. The temperature contrasts are fun, and the meal is so nutritious and satisfying.

Bring a medium pot of water to a boil over high heat. Add the rice and boil (like pasta) until tender, about 40 minutes, then remove the pot from the heat. Drain the rice and return it to the pot. Cover and allow it to steam for 5 minutes. Uncover the pot and fluff the rice gently with a fork. Re-cover and set aside.

Prepare the marinated kale. Place the kale in a large bowl. In a small bowl, whisk together the olive oil, vinegar, mustard, garlic powder, maple syrup, and salt. Pour this mixture over the kale. Use your hands to "massage" the dressing into the kale for a couple minutes, until the leaves are well coated and softened. Cover the bowl and transfer to the fridge.

Heat the avocado oil in a large nonstick skillet over medium heat. Add the onion and cook for 5 to 6 minutes, stirring frequently, until softening and becoming translucent. Add the bell pepper and mushrooms to the skillet and continue sautéing the vegetables, stirring frequently, for another 7 to 10 minutes, until the pepper is soft and the mushrooms have released their liquid. Reduce the heat to low.

In a small bowl, whisk together the tahini, water, lemon juice, mustard, and liquid aminos.

Crumble the tofu into the skillet with your hands. (You can crumble it fine or leave some sizable chunks, as preferred.) Pour the tahini mixture over the tofu. Stir the tofu and vegetables well, mixing them with the tahini sauce. Then, sprinkle the nutritional yeast, turmeric, paprika, and kala namak over the scramble. Continue stirring the ingredients gently

for 2 minutes, until the tofu is heated through. If the tofu looks a bit dry, add a tablespoon or two of water. Taste the scramble and add additional salt and pepper as desired.

Divide the cooked rice and tofu scramble among four bowls or place in separate airtight storage containers. Add one-fourth of the kale to each bowl, then mix and enjoy. The salad can be stored for up to 4 days in the fridge.

½ teaspoon ground turmeric

¼ teaspoon smoked paprika

¼ teaspoon kala namak (Himalayan black salt) or fine sea salt, or more as needed

Freshly ground black pepper

Place any of my favorite ingredients between two slices of bread and I'm guaranteed to love them all the more. I'm a sandwich enthusiast, and it's only fitting for me to devote a chapter of this book to green and bean combinations that are sandwiched between, or piled on top of, bready things.

Open-faced recipes include classic avocado toasts with briny kimchi and tender adzuki beans (see page 85); English muffins with saucy cannellini beans and Tuscan kale (see page 90); a tray of toasted pita chips topped with heaps of crispy chickpeas, roasted broccolini, and herbed tahini sauce (see page 81); and savory mini-waffles smothered in spiced kidney beans and greens (see page 82).

The eleven "closed" recipes are mostly sandwiches, but include two stuffed pita pockets and a folded, toasted tortilla, quesadilla-style (see page 117). If you love the classics, then a vegan spin on caprese, prepared with marinated tofu in place of mozzarella (see page 97) might be for you. For something more surprising, you may fall in love with wedges of creamy roasted kabocha squash, piled on top of a garlicky white bean spread and garnished with peppery arugula (see page 110).

The "bread" in the chapter title doesn't only denote bread. It includes wheat wraps and tortillas, homemade, crispy cornmeal and flour waffles, and pita. So many breads, flatbreads, and pancakes are used around the world to sop up, scoop up, and sandwich various beans and greens; this section offers only a tiny sampling of them. Once you start to conceptualize bread, beans, and greens as a self-sufficient meal, there will be so many options to explore. You might find that a lot of your favorite sandwiches already fit the formula.

For each of the recipes, I offer a suggested type of bread. Sometimes there's a strong case for using one type rather than another; for example, the baked tempeh and sauerkraut, which is reminiscent of a Reuben sandwich, calls for pumpernickel or rye. However, for the most part, the sandwich breads I suggest can be substituted with something you have at home.

BEANS & GREENS ON BREAD

SAUTÉED BUTTER BEANS, LEEKS, AND ESCAROLE

Makes 4 servings

Grain: sourdough bread
Green: escarole
Bean: butter beans

———————

2 tablespoons extra-virgin olive oil

3 leeks, white parts only, trimmed, sliced crosswise into ½-inch / 1.3cm pieces, cleaned thoroughly

2 garlic cloves, minced

1 large head escarole, trimmed and chopped into bite-sized pieces

1½ cups / 360ml vegetable broth

3 cups / 480g cooked butter beans, or 2 (15-ounce / 425g) cans butter beans, drained and rinsed

½ teaspoon salt, or more as needed

1½ tablespoons white balsamic vinegar, or more as needed

Red pepper flakes, for serving

8 slices sourdough bread (or other bread), for toasting

We didn't eat a lot of alliums when I was growing up, so I warmed up to them slowly on my journey to becoming a home cook. Leeks, however, won me over quickly. They're inherently milder and sweeter than onions, and I love how creamy they become with cooking. In this recipe, leeks and escarole are sautéed until almost meltingly tender and quite sweet, then are mixed with plump butter beans. There are wonderful and distinctive layers of texture here: silky-soft vegetables, creamy beans, and crispy toast. This is a great winter lunch, which can be made a little spicy if you're liberal with the red pepper flakes.

Heat the olive oil in a large, deep skillet over medium heat. When the oil is shimmering, add the leeks. Sauté the leeks for 7 to 8 minutes, stirring a few times, until tender and translucent. Add the garlic. Continue to cook the leeks with the garlic for 2 more minutes, stirring frequently, until the garlic is fragrant.

Add the escarole to the skillet in handfuls. Cook, stirring frequently, for 3 minutes. (You may need to wilt it in batches to get all the greens to fit in the skillet.) Add the broth to the skillet, bring it to a simmer, cover the skillet, and turn the heat to low. Simmer for 6 to 8 minutes, until the escarole is uniformly tender.

Uncover the skillet and stir in the butter beans, salt, and vinegar. Continue to simmer, uncovered, for 3 more minutes, until the butter beans are warmed through. Taste the mixture and add additional salt and vinegar as desired, as well as the red pepper flakes to taste.

Toast the bread and arrange two slices on each of four plates. Top each serving with one-fourth of the bean mixture. To eat, pick up the slices and enjoy them by the (deliciously messy!) bite, or dive into the toasts with a knife and fork. The greens and bean mixture can be stored for up to 5 days in an airtight container in the fridge.

PITA CHIPS AND CRISPY CHICKPEAS
WITH BROCCOLINI AND GREEN TAHINI SAUCE

Makes 4 servings

Grain: pita pockets
Green: broccolini
Bean: chickpeas

---

2 white or whole-wheat pita pockets

1 tablespoon and 1½ tablespoons avocado oil, divided

Salt

1 large or 2 small bunches fresh baby broccoli (broccolini), cut into 2½-inch / 6cm pieces

Red pepper flakes

¾ cup / 180ml Green Tahini Sauce (page 216)

1½ cups / 140g Crispy Chickpeas (page 209)

1 cup / 130g Quick Pickled Onions (page 208)

½ cup / 20g chopped fresh parsley

This is a great dish to make for friends, as it's easy to serve family style. Rather than creating individual pitas, you'll make a big batch of crispy pita chips, then treat them sort of like the tortilla chips for a batch of nachos. Layer them with heaps of roasted baby broccoli, crispy chickpeas, pickled onions, and herbs, then smother them with green tahini sauce.

Preheat the oven to 425°F / 220°C.

Split the pitas in half crosswise, so that each pocket becomes two flat rounds. Stack the rounds and cut them into quarters (16 pieces). Spread the pieces on a sheet pan. Use some of the 1 tablespoon avocado oil to brush the tops of the pieces lightly. (Alternatively, use avocado oil cooking spray.) Sprinkle the pita wedges with salt.

Line another sheet pan with aluminum foil or use a nonstick sheet pan. Spread the broccoli on the prepared sheet pan and drizzle with the remaining 1½ tablespoons avocado oil. Sprinkle the broccoli with a generous pinch of salt and the red pepper flakes to taste.

Transfer both sheet pans to the oven. Bake the pita chips for 3 to 5 minutes, until their tops are just browning. Flip the pita pieces, brush or spray them again with the remaining avocado oil, and sprinkle with salt. Bake for another 3 to 5 minutes, until crispy and browning on both sides, but not burnt. Meanwhile, roast the broccoli for about 15 minutes, until browning and turning crispy.

Arrange the baked pita chips on a serving platter or plate that's large enough to hold them all in a single layer. Spoon about half the tahini sauce over the pita chips. Pile the broccoli and roasted chickpeas on the chips, then pour the remaining tahini sauce over them, or as much sauce as you'd like to add. Top the loaded chips with the pickled onions and sprinkle with the parsley, then serve right away. To prepare this ahead of time, make the components in advance, then reheat the chips, chickpeas, and baby broccoli in a 350°F / 175°C oven for 10 minutes, until crispy and warm. Assemble to serve. The chips, chickpeas, broccoli, and sauce will keep in separate airtight containers in the fridge for up to 4 days.

Makes 4 servings

Grain: corn waffles
Green: kale
Bean: red kidney beans

_____

1½ cups / 240g cooked
dark red kidney beans, or
1 (15-ounce / 425g) can
kidney beans, drained
and rinsed

1 cup / 240g salsa of choice
(mild or hot, chunky or
smooth, green or red)

1 small bunch curly kale,
stemmed and chopped

WAFFLES

1 cup / 120g unbleached
all-purpose flour

¾ cup / 105g medium-grind
cornmeal

1 teaspoon baking powder

¼ teaspoon baking soda

¼ teaspoon salt

1 cup / 240ml unsweetened
soy, oat, almond, or cashew
milk

1 tablespoon freshly
squeezed lemon juice, apple
cider vinegar, or distilled
white vinegar

1 tablespoon avocado oil

OPTIONAL TOPPINGS

Sliced or chopped Hass
avocado

Additional salsa

Halved cherry tomatoes

Chopped fresh cilantro
or green onions, green
parts only

Pickled jalapeños

SAVORY CORN WAFFLES
WITH KIDNEY BEANS AND KALE

Beans, greens, bread, and a store-bought simmering sauce is the
perfect formula for a "semi-homemade" lunch. I use red sauce for
my Tuscan-inspired marinara beans and kale (see page 90), and for
this recipe, I use salsa, which instantly seasons kidney beans and
curly kale. Those ingredients are piled onto crispy, savory mini corn
waffles, which are a delightful alternative to bread. The corn waffles
can be frozen for future breakfasts or lunches, and I've found that
they work with all sorts of toppings, such as traditional baked beans,
pieces of Eggy Tofu (page 212), and Guacamole (page 221). Note: This
recipe yields 8 mini waffles, each about 4 inches / 10cm in diameter.
However, you can also prepare 4 Belgian-style round waffles or 4 to
6 square waffles instead, depending on the shape of the waffle iron
you have.

Combine the beans and salsa in a large, deep skillet and bring to a
simmer over medium-low heat. Add the kale, cover the skillet, and
simmer for 10 to 12 minutes, stirring every few minutes, until the kale
is tender. Remove the skillet from the heat, cover, and set aside.

Prepare the waffles. Preheat a waffle iron on high. In a large bowl, whisk
together the flour, cornmeal, baking powder, baking soda, and salt. In
a medium bowl, whisk together the non-dairy milk and lemon juice,
then stir in the avocado oil. Pour the wet ingredients into the dry and
mix until combined into a mostly smooth batter. There should be no
streaks of flour visible in the batter, but a few lumps are fine.

Transfer the waffle batter to the waffle iron using a ¼ cup / 60ml
measure for mini-waffles or a ⅔ cup / 160ml measure for large waffles.
Cook the waffles until golden and crispy on the outside, according
to the manufacturer's instructions.

To serve, place a small heap of the bean and kale mixture on each mini
waffle, then add your toppings of choice. The beans and kale will keep
for up to 4 days in an airtight container in the fridge. The waffles will
keep in an airtight container in the fridge for up to 2 days and can be
frozen for up to 6 weeks.

ADZUKI BEANS, KIMCHI, AND MASHED AVOCADO

Makes 4 servings

Grain: sourdough bread
Green: kimchi
Bean: adzuki beans

_____

2 large or 3 small ripe Hass avocados

2 teaspoons toasted white sesame seeds

2 teaspoons black sesame seeds (or additional white sesame seeds)

1 teaspoon nori flakes, or 1 sheet toasted, salted nori, crumbled finely

½ teaspoon ground ginger

1 tablespoon freshly squeezed lime juice

Red pepper flakes

Salt

8 slices sourdough bread (or other bread)

1 cup / 160g cooked adzuki or black beans

8 ounces / 225g vegan kimchi, chopped (mild, regular, or spicy)

These toasts are simple enough to put together for lunch on a busy WFH day, yet they're more complex and satisfying than the classic, plain avocado toast that inspires them. Kimchi adds savoriness and the tangy, funky flavor that's common among fermented foods. If you find kimchi to be too spicy, know that there are now many store-bought vegan kimchi options, and they have a range of heat levels and flavor profiles. Adding crushed nori, salt, red pepper flakes, and ginger to the avocado is a nod to togarashi spice, and you can substitute a couple teaspoons of store-bought togarashi for the seasoning blend if you have it. I most often make this toast recipe with adzuki beans, but black beans are a great substitute.

Cut the avocados open and remove their pits. Scoop the flesh of the avocados into a medium bowl. Mash roughly with a fork, then add the sesame seeds, nori, ginger, and lime juice. Continue mixing and mashing the avocado until you have a chunky mixture similar to guacamole. Add the red pepper flakes and salt to taste.

Toast the sourdough, if desired. Spread some of the avocado mixture on each of the eight slices. Top each with 2 tablespoons of the adzuki beans, then 2 tablespoons (1 ounce / 30g) of the kimchi. Enjoy right away—this toast recipe is best served fresh!

EGGY TOFU AND SAUTÉED SPINACH

Makes 4 servings

Grain: English muffins

Green: spinach

Bean: tofu

_____

DIJONNAISE SAUCE

½ cup / 120ml Cashew Sour Cream (page 216) or store-bought vegan mayonnaise

1 tablespoon nutritional yeast

1 tablespoon Dijon mustard

⅛ teaspoon ground turmeric

¼ cup / 60ml water

Freshly squeezed lemon juice (optional)

Freshly ground black pepper

1 tablespoon olive oil

2 garlic cloves, very thinly sliced

8 ounces / 225g fresh baby spinach leaves or roughly chopped spinach leaves and stems (about 8 cups)

⅛ teaspoon salt

4 English muffins

8 slices Eggy Tofu (page 212)

The inspiration for this open-faced English muffin is eggs florentine, which combines a poached egg with sautéed spinach and hollandaise sauce. In place of the egg, the protein here is pan-fried slabs of Eggy Tofu, stained a pale yellow with ground turmeric. I like to add Dijon mustard to the dairy-free sauce, resulting in something that's a little punchier than traditional hollandaise—I'm calling it "dijonnaise," which is a nod to a condiment I loved growing up. These sandwiches are an excellent weekend brunch option, but if you make the components ahead of time, they can be a great work-from-home lunch, too.

Prepare the sauce. In a small bowl or liquid measuring cup, stir together the Cashew Sour Cream, nutritional yeast, mustard, turmeric, and water. Taste and add a squeeze of lemon juice (if using; if you use Cashew Sour Cream, you may not need additional acid). Add the black pepper to taste.

Place the olive oil in a large, deep skillet over medium-low heat. When the oil is shimmering, add the garlic to the skillet. Sauté, stirring constantly, for 30 seconds, until the garlic is fragrant and a few edges are just starting to brown. Add the spinach to the skillet in handfuls, stirring as you go; this will help to wilt the spinach quickly and create room in the pan for adding all the spinach. Sauté the spinach for about 2 minutes, until wilted and tender but still vividly green. Add the salt and stir to incorporate. Use tongs or a spatula to remove the spinach from the skillet, allowing any excess liquid to drain off.

Split and toast the English muffins. Distribute the sautéed spinach over each of the 8 toasted muffin halves. Arrange a slice of tofu on top of each. Drizzle a tablespoon of the sauce over each muffin half. Enjoy the muffins, two halves per person. The tofu slices and sauce will keep in separate airtight containers in the fridge for up to 4 days. The spinach will keep in another airtight container in the fridge for up to 3 days.

MAPLE MUSTARD LENTILS, SWEET POTATOES, AND HERBS

Makes 4 servings

Grain: whole-grain bread
Green: chives, parsley, baby arugula (optional)
Bean: green lentils

_____

If you enjoy sweet and savory seasoning combinations as much as I do, you'll love the spicy-tangy and sweet-salty mix of maple syrup and Dijon mustard. In this recipe, they're turned into a creamy dressing with the addition of tahini and savory liquid aminos. Together, these flavors are bold enough to stand up to the earthiness of the lentils and sweet potatoes, making a hearty topping for open-faced, whole-grain toasts. The green component in this recipe is chopped fresh herbs—chives and parsley—plus some baby arugula. They give a welcome sense of freshness and offer specks of color.

1 cup / 200g dried green lentils, picked over

2 sweet potatoes, peeled and cut into ½-inch / 1.3cm cubes (about 1 pound / 455g)

1 large or 2 small shallots, trimmed and minced

¼ cup / 10g snipped fresh chives

2 tablespoons chopped fresh parsley

¼ cup / 60g tahini

2 tablespoons Dijon mustard, or more as needed

2½ tablespoons Bragg Liquid Aminos or tamari, or more as needed

2½ tablespoons apple cider vinegar, or more as needed

2 tablespoons water

8 slices whole-grain bread

Roughly chopped baby arugula or additional chopped parsley, for serving (optional)

Bring a medium pot of water to a boil over medium-high heat and add the lentils. Boil the lentils for 15 to 25 minutes, until tender but retaining their shape and some firmness. Drain the lentils through a fine-mesh strainer. Using tea towels or paper towels, press the lentils gently through the strainer to help remove all excess moisture. Set the lentils aside.

Fill the same pot with a few inches of water and fit it with a steamer attachment. Bring the water to a simmer over medium-low heat. Add the sweet potatoes and steam for 10 minutes, until tender.

Place the sweet potatoes, lentils, shallots, chives, and parsley in a large mixing bowl.

In a small bowl or liquid measuring cup, whisk together the tahini, mustard, liquid aminos, vinegar, and water. Pour this dressing over the lentil and sweet potato mixture. Mix well, then adjust the mustard, liquid aminos, and vinegar to taste.

Toast the bread, if desired. Divide the lentils and sweet potatoes among the toasts—2 slices per serving—and top the slices with a bit of the arugula or additional parsley (if using). The lentil and sweet potato mixture will keep in an airtight container in the fridge for up to 4 days.

Makes 4 servings

Grain: English muffins
Green: kale
Bean: cannellini beans

———

1½ cups / 280g cooked cannellini beans, or 1 (15-ounce / 425g) can cannellini beans, drained

1½ cups / 360ml store-bought marinara sauce (such as Rao's)

1 small bunch Tuscan kale, stemmed, leaves sliced crosswise into thin ribbons

4 English muffins

Cheesy Topping (page 209) or store-bought vegan parmesan cheese, for topping (or mozzarella-style vegan cheese shreds)

MARINARA WHITE BEAN AND KALE ENGLISH MUFFINS

This recipe is a tribute to a childhood favorite—pizza English muffins—but with a slightly more grown-up persona. The greens and beans (Tuscan kale and cannellini beans) are simmered with store-bought marinara sauce, then piled onto toasted English muffins and sprinkled with my Cheesy Topping. This is more of a meal idea than a recipe, and it's open to creative interpretation. For example, you can stir in some rehydrated TVP for extra protein, or you could cover the saucy beans and greens with some plant-based mozzarella shreds, then pop the English muffins under the broiler for a couple minutes before serving. I like to use a sturdy English muffin, such as the sprouted-grain muffins from the Food for Life brand, and I'm unwavering in my devotion to the Rao's brand of marinara sauce.

Combine the beans and sauce in a large, deep skillet and bring to a simmer over medium-low heat. Add the kale, cover the skillet, and simmer for 10 to 12 minutes, stirring every few minutes, until the kale is tender.

Split and toast the English muffins. On each of four plates, top two halves with one-fourth of the saucy bean mixture, then sprinkle with the Cheesy Topping as desired. Leftover beans and greens will keep for up to 5 days in an airtight container in the fridge.

SAUCY RED PEPPER BUTTER BEANS AND SPINACH WITH WARM PITA WEDGES

Makes 4 servings

Grain: pita breads
Green: spinach
Bean: butter beans

This bean, green, and bread meal is one of the best recipes you can make with my Red Pepper Sauce. I love that this recipe requires no chopping or sautéing of vegetables. You simply combine the sauce and two cans of butter beans in a skillet, bring the sauce to a simmer, and wilt in some baby spinach. While you do that, you can heat some fluffy pita bread in the oven. Cut the warm pita into soft wedges and use those pieces to scoop up the saucy bean mixture. I recommend serving this dish with a big green salad for a relaxed summer supper, or you can enjoy it as is for a quick and easy lunch.

Preheat the oven to 325°F / 165°C. Wrap the pitas in foil and let them warm in the oven while you proceed with the recipe.

Combine the sauce and beans in a large skillet. Bring the sauce to a simmer, then turn the heat to low. Simmer the beans, uncovered, for 5 minutes, until the sauce has thickened a little. Add the spinach, stirring as you go, until wilted, 1 to 2 minutes, then allow the greens to simmer with the beans for another 2 minutes, until the spinach is tender. Add some harissa paste to taste.

Divide the saucy beans and greens among four bowls. Cut the pitas into quarters and serve four quarters with each bowl, for scooping. The saucy beans and greens will keep in an airtight container in the fridge for up to 4 days.

4 white or whole-wheat pita breads or pocketless pitas (such as Angel brand pocketless)

1 batch (2 cups / 480ml) Red Pepper Sauce (page 214)

3 cups / 480g cooked butter beans, or 2 (15-ounce / 425g) cans butter beans, drained and rinsed

5 ounces / 150g fresh baby spinach

1 to 2 tablespoons harissa paste (or generous pinch of red pepper flakes)

FRENCH ONION BROTHY BEANS AND GREENS WITH GARLIC TOAST

Makes 4 servings

Grain: sourdough bread
Green: dark leafy greens
Bean: cannellini beans

_____

2 tablespoons olive oil, plus more for brushing on the toast

3 or 4 large sweet onions (1¾ to 2 pounds / 800 to 900g), halved lengthwise and cut into ³⁄₁₆- to ¼-inch / 4 to 6mm slices

½ teaspoon salt, or more as needed

2 teaspoons brown sugar or cane sugar

2 garlic cloves, minced

½ cup / 60ml dry white wine (or additional broth)

1½ tablespoons white balsamic vinegar (or red)

1 cup / 240ml vegetable broth or vegan beef-style broth

3 cups / 480g cooked cannellini beans, or 2 (15-ounce / 425g) cans cannellini beans, drained

4 cups / 80g stemmed and chopped dark leafy greens (such as Swiss chard, curly or Tuscan kale, spinach, or broccoli rabe)

Freshly ground black pepper

8 small or 4 large slices sourdough bread

1 large garlic clove, cut in half

I've always had a weakness for French onion soup. It's one of the first dishes I can remember eating at a fancy restaurant with my mother and grandmother, both Francophiles when it came to food, and this toast is a tribute dish. I know there are lots of hacks for speeding up the process of caramelizing onions, but so far I haven't found one that beats just summoning up a little patience and giving the onions time. I like to serve the beans over oven-toasted sourdough slices that have been rubbed with garlic and brushed with olive oil. For a traditional onion soup twist, melt some plant-based cheese on top of the beans just before serving.

Heat the olive oil in a large, deep skillet (which has a lid) over medium-high heat. Add the onions and salt and stir to coat the onion slices with the oil. Cover the skillet and cook on high heat for 5 minutes. Uncover the skillet, stir the onions, and add the brown sugar. Reduce the heat to medium-low and re-cover the pot. Continue cooking the onions until caramelized, anywhere from 25 to 45 minutes. Uncover the skillet and stir every 8 minutes. You should start to see some browned bits in the bottom of the skillet as the onions caramelize, which you'll stir into the mixture. However, if you see a lot of blackened or burned areas, reduce the heat to slow the cooking. When they've finished caramelizing, the onions should be a deep golden brown, meltingly tender, and reduced considerably in size.

Add the garlic to the skillet. Cook the onions and garlic, stirring constantly, for 1 minute. Add the wine and vinegar to the skillet and give the onions a stir to deglaze the pan. Allow the liquid to come to a simmer and cook, uncovered, for 5 to 7 minutes, until the wine has mostly cooked off.

Add the broth, beans, and greens to the skillet. Cover the skillet and allow the broth to come to a simmer. When it does, uncover the skillet and simmer the beans, greens, and onions, uncovered, for 5 minutes, until they have thickened a bit but are still liquidy. Taste the mixture. Add black pepper to taste and additional salt as needed.

To prepare the toast, turn the broiler to high. Line a sheet pan with aluminum foil or use a nonstick sheet pan. Place the bread slices on the

prepared sheet pan and toast in the broiler for 2 to 3 minutes on each side, flipping halfway through, until they're golden brown on both sides.

Brush the slices with a little olive oil. Rub the cut side of the garlic on the oiled slices. Place the toast on plates, two slices per plate. To serve, divide the warm beans among the four plates of toast. The beans can be stored in an airtight container in the fridge for up to 6 days and frozen for up to 8 weeks.

TOFU, PESTO, AND TOMATO CAPRESE

Makes 4 servings

Grain: ciabatta rolls
Green: basil
Bean: tofu

———————

Caprese sandwiches were always a favorite of mine growing up. In creating a vegan version, I asked myself what could be a tangy, creamy, salty replacement for mozzarella, and I found the answer to be slabs of Cheesy Tofu. The green component in these sandwiches is a healthy amount of vegan Pesto, along with fresh basil leaves. If you'd like to add even more green, you could top your sandwiches with baby arugula or spinach, or you could add slices of grilled zucchini. Ciabatta rolls are my first choice for the sandwiches, but if you have a hard time finding them, use toasted sourdough bread, an Italian-style roll, or pieces of vegan focaccia that have been sliced in half crosswise.

Spread four halves of the ciabatta each with 2 tablespoons pesto. Top each with two slabs of the Cheesy Tofu, one slice of tomato, and a layer of basil leaves. If you're a fan of balsamic vinegar, drizzle some syrupy balsamic over the basil leaves. Top the sandwiches with the remaining halves, then serve.

4 ciabatta rolls, sliced in half crosswise (or 8 slices toasted sourdough bread, or 4 [4-inch / 10cm] square pieces vegan focaccia bread, sliced in half crosswise)

½ cup / 125ml Pesto (page 217)

8 pieces Cheesy Tofu (page 210), marinated in slabs

4 (¼-inch / 6mm) slices ripe heirloom or beefsteak tomato

1 cup / 12g lightly packed fresh basil

Aged balsamic vinegar (optional)

Makes 4 servings

Grain: pita þockets

Green: arugula

Bean: lentils

_____

⅓ cup / 55g golden raisins

⅓ cup / 80ml white wine vinegar, or more as needed

1 large cauliflower, cut into bite-sized florets and pieces (about 1½ pounds / 680g)

1½ tablespoons and 2 tablespoons olive oil, divided, or more as needed

2 teaspoons grated lemon zest (approximately of 1 lemon)

1½ tablespoons freshly squeezed lemon juice

Salt

Red pepper flakes

2 tablespoons pine nuts

1 garlic clove, finely minced or grated

2 tablespoons drained capers

1¾ cups / 265g cooked green, brown, black, or French lentils, or 1 (15-ounce / 425g) can lentils, drained and rinsed

6 cups / 120g lightly packed baby arugula

4 white or whole-wheat pita pockets

SICILIAN-STYLE ROASTED CAULIFLOWER, LENTILS, AND ARUGULA

Sicilian-style cauliflower combines crispy roasted cauliflower florets with capers, red pepper flakes, pine nuts, golden raisins, lemon juice, and parsley. It's a tangy, salty, spicy flavor bomb, and while it makes an excellent side dish, the cauliflower is also a great filling for a pita pocket. I add lentils for protein, and the green in this recipe is arugula, which adds a peppery crunch. French or black lentils are my preference for the pita pockets, but green or brown lentils are fine, too.

In a small bowl, combine the raisins and vinegar. Allow the raisins to soak while you proceed with the recipe.

Preheat the oven to 425°F / 220°C. Line a sheet pan with parchment paper or aluminum foil or use a nonstick sheet pan.

Place the cauliflower on the prepared sheet pan. Add 1½ tablespoons of the olive oil, the lemon zest and juice, and a generous pinch each of salt and red pepper flakes. Mix the cauliflower well to coat it with oil and seasonings. Roast the cauliflower for 30 to 35 minutes, until tender and turning golden and crispy. Stir the cauliflower once halfway through roasting. In the last 5 minutes of roasting, add the pine nuts to the sheet pan and toast them a little while the cauliflower finishes cooking.

When the cauliflower has finished roasting, drain the raisins and place on a plate, reserving 1½ tablespoons of the vinegar in the bowl. Whisk in the remaining 2 tablespoons olive oil, ¼ teaspoon salt, and the garlic.

Place the roasted cauliflower and pine nuts in a large bowl. Add the raisins, the capers, lentils, and arugula, then add the olive oil and vinegar mixture. Toss the ingredients well to combine. Taste and add additional oil, vinegar, salt, or red pepper flakes as desired.

Cut the four pita pockets in half. Divide the cauliflower mixture among the halves and serve 2 halves per person. The cauliflower mixture will keep in an airtight container in the fridge for up to 4 days.

BAKED TEMPEH SLICES AND SAUERKRAUT

Makes 4 sandwiches

Grain: marbled rye bread
Green: sauerkraut
(green cabbage)
Bean: tempeh

Salty baked tempeh, a creamy pink dressing, sauerkraut, and rye bread—yes, this is my take on the Reuben sandwich. Instead of a small mountain of pastrami, though, I use tempeh slices that have been marinated in lemon juice and black pepper. These slices are versatile enough to work well in a BLT or any other "meaty" sandwich or wrap. I like to use caraway-flavored sauerkraut and marbled rye bread for this humble tribute to one of the great deli sandwiches of all time.

Arrange the tempeh slices in one or two layers in a rectangular storage container with an airtight lid.

In a small bowl or liquid measuring cup, whisk together the liquid aminos, avocado oil, lemon juice, agave nectar, onion powder, paprika, and black pepper. Pour this marinade over the tempeh. Cover the container tightly and shake it a little to distribute the marinade. Place the container in the fridge and marinate for at least 2 hours and up to overnight.

Preheat the oven to 375°F / 190°C. Line a sheet pan with parchment paper or use a nonstick sheet pan.

Remove the tempeh pieces from their marinade, reserving the marinade. Arrange the tempeh slices flat on the prepared sheet pan. Brush the slices with the marinade. Bake the tempeh for 10 minutes, then flip the slices over and brush again with marinade. Bake for another 5 to 8 minutes, until the slices are browning lightly on both sides.

Meanwhile, prepare the dressing. In a small bowl or liquid measuring cup, combine the Cashew Sour Cream, ketchup, relish, vinegar, chili powder, and shallot (if using). Mix well, then add the horseradish to taste (if using).

Spread 1 tablespoon of the dressing on each of four pieces of rye. Arrange one-fourth of the tempeh slices on top, then add ⅓ cup / 45g of the sauerkraut to each. Top the sandwiches with the remaining bread slices. Alternatively, you can toast the bread before assembling your sandwiches. Enjoy. The tempeh slices will keep in an airtight container in the fridge for up to 4 days. The dressing will keep for up to 3 days.

1 (8-ounce / 225g) block tempeh, sliced crosswise into ¼-inch / 6mm slices

2 tablespoons Bragg Liquid Aminos or tamari

1 tablespoon avocado oil

¼ cup / 60ml freshly squeezed lemon juice

2 teaspoons agave nectar or pure maple syrup

½ teaspoon onion powder

¼ teaspoon smoked paprika

¼ teaspoon freshly ground black pepper

RUSSIAN-STYLE DRESSING

½ cup / 120ml Cashew Sour Cream (page 216) or store-bought vegan mayonnaise

2 tablespoons ketchup

2 tablespoons sweet relish

1 teaspoon apple cider vinegar

¼ teaspoon chili powder or paprika

1 tablespoon minced shallot or white onion (optional)

1 to 2 teaspoons prepared horseradish (optional)

1⅓ cups / 160g caraway-flavored sauerkraut (or plain sauerkraut)

8 slices marbled rye bread, plain rye bread, or sandwich bread

Makes 4 servings

Grain: bread of choice
Green: cucumber, arugula
Bean: black beans

_____

1½ cups / 240g cooked black beans, or 1 (15-ounce / 425g) can black beans, drained

½ teaspoon salt

1½ tablespoons freshly squeezed lime juice, plus extra as needed

Freshly ground black pepper

8 slices bread of choice

1 large Hass avocado, pitted and cut into quarters

1 seedless cucumber, peeled and sliced thinly crosswise

1 ripe beefsteak tomato, cut crosswise into ¼-inch / 6mm slices

1 cup / 20g fresh baby arugula

1 cup / 130g loosely packed Quick Pickled Onions (page 208)

BLACK BEANS, PICKLED ONIONS, CUCUMBER, AND AVOCADO

One of the joys of life in this digital age is a constant influx of inspiration from online friends. Joseph Suarez, who goes by the handle @Joesveganfoodgram on Instagram, is one of my go-to sources for vegan sandwiches, inspired by discoveries in his hometown of Los Angeles. One of Joe's regular picks is a vegan version of the Green Lab sandwich from an eatery called The Food Lab. I've never tasted this sandwich myself, but Joe's photos inspired me to create a version of my own with mashed black beans, cucumber, tomato, avocado, arugula, and pickled onions. Enjoy this vibrant combination in the summer, when the tomatoes and cucumbers are fresh, and be generous with the pickled onions, which give the sandwich a lot of personality.

In a small bowl, add the beans and use a potato masher or the back of a spoon to mash them. You can leave the mixture with a lot of texture or make it a more uniform mash, depending on your preferences. Stir in the salt, lime juice, and black pepper to taste.

Toast the bread. Spoon one-fourth of the avocado onto each of four slices. Use a fork to roughly mash the avocado onto the toast, then drizzle each with a squeeze of lime juice.

Spread the black bean mash onto the remaining four slices. Top each of these with one-fourth of the cucumber and tomato slices, the arugula, and pickled onions. Gently top these slices with each of the avocado toasts. Cut the sandwiches in half and enjoy.

ANTIPASTO CANNELLINI BEANS AND SPINACH

Makes 4 servings

Grain: pita pockets
Green: artichokes, baby spinach
Bean: cannellini beans

——————

Do you have a leftover half can of beans? A handful or two of salad greens or leftover broccoli florets? An almost empty jar of roasted red bell peppers or olives? Put them into a pita pocket! Stuffed pita pockets are one of my all-time favorite, easy lunches, and they're a perfect way to use up those odds and ends. This recipe features a couple of the briny, pickled items that tend to live in my pantry—jarred sun-dried tomatoes and marinated artichoke quarters—as well as cannellini beans and some fresh baby spinach. The combo captures the flavors I love from classic antipasti offerings, and it's incredibly easy to make. Sometimes I add some Red Pepper Hummus (page 219) to the pita pockets before stuffing them.

Place the beans, artichoke hearts, sun-dried tomatoes, red peppers, and baby spinach in a large bowl. Add the vinegar and mix well. Drizzle olive oil over the mixture as desired, along with salt and pepper to taste.

Use this mixture to stuff the pita pocket halves, two halves per person. Enjoy. The bean and vegetable mixture will keep in an airtight container in the fridge for up to 3 days.

1½ cups / 280g cooked cannellini beans, or 1 (14.5-ounce / 415g) can cannellini beans, drained and rinsed

1½ cups / 400g quartered artichoke hearts, or 1 (14-ounce / 400g) can artichoke hearts, drained

6 tablespoons / 90g chopped oil-packed sun-dried tomatoes

½ cup / 100g roughly chopped jarred roasted red bell peppers

4 cups / 80g fresh baby spinach

1½ tablespoons red wine vinegar

Olive oil

Salt and freshly ground black pepper

4 white or whole-wheat pita pockets, halved vertically

Makes 4 servings

Grain: soft sandwich bread
Green: butter lettuce
Bean: tofu

————————

1 (14-ounce / 400g) block
extra-firm tofu, pressed
(see page 212)

6 tablespoons / 90ml
Cashew Sour Cream
(page 216) or store-bought
vegan sour cream

2 tablespoons Dijon mustard

½ teaspoon kala namak
(Himalayan black salt) or
fine sea salt

½ teaspoon ground turmeric

⅓ cup / 35g finely diced
celery

2 tablespoons finely chopped
fresh chives

8 slices sandwich bread
of choice

12 large butter lettuce leaves

TURMERIC TOFU AND
BUTTER LETTUCE

When tofu is mixed or marinated with turmeric and black salt, it takes on a golden hue and eggy flavor. When that same tofu is crumbled, it has a texture that's perfect for replicating scrambled eggs or egg salad—with a similarly high protein content to boot. If you love a good, old-fashioned egg salad sandwich, then there's a good chance you'll fall in love with this plant-based interpretation. The creamy dressing for crumbled tofu is a mixture of Cashew Sour Cream, Dijon mustard, chives, and turmeric, which lends its characteristic yellow color. If you don't have a batch of homemade sour cream at the ready, it's fine to use store-bought vegan mayo instead; I love the Vegenaise brand. I like to keep this sandwich simple: just the tofu, soft sandwich bread, and a few big pieces of butter lettuce, which are this meal's green.

In a medium bowl, combine the tofu, Cashew Sour Cream, mustard, black salt, and turmeric. Use your hands to finely crumble the tofu and thoroughly mix it with the seasonings until you have a uniform mixture. There can be a little texture, but you're not aiming to have larger pieces of tofu in this recipe. Add the celery and chives and continue mixing until the green bits are evenly incorporated.

Top four of the slices with one-fourth each of the tofu mixture, followed by 3 lettuce leaves, then top with another slice of bread. Alternatively, toast the bread before assembling your sandwiches. Slice each sandwich in half and enjoy. The turmeric tofu will keep in an airtight container in the fridge for up to 4 days.

BARBECUE TEMPEH AND SLAW

Makes 4 servings

Grain: burger buns
Green: green cabbage
Bean: tempeh

Here's a fun vegan option for all your summer outdoor gatherings: burger buns piled high with sweet, tender slabs of barbecue tempeh and a creamy, crispy vegan coleslaw. I'll take the texture contrast, color, and nutrition of this meal over a ubiquitous veggie burger any day!

Make the tempeh. Fill a medium pot with a few inches of water, then fit it with a steamer attachment. Bring the water to a boil over high heat. Cut the tempeh in half crosswise. Cut each of those pieces in half lengthwise, then widthwise, so you have 8 rectangles in total. Steam the tempeh pieces for 10 minutes. Transfer the steamed tempeh to a rectangular storage container with a lid.

In a small bowl, whisk together the tomato paste, water, liquid aminos, oil, maple syrup, vinegar, molasses, paprika, and chili powder. Pour this sauce over the tempeh pieces. Flip them around so all the various sides are coated with the marinade. Cover the container and place in the fridge for at least 4 hours and up to overnight.

Preheat the oven to 375°F / 190°C. Line a sheet pan with parchment paper or use a nonstick sheet pan.

Remove the tempeh pieces from their marinade and arrange them on the prepared sheet pan. Bake the tempeh for 10 minutes, then flip the slices over. Bake for another 10 minutes, until the slices look darkened and are just browning at the edges.

Prepare the slaw. Place the cabbages and carrots in a large bowl. In a small bowl or liquid measuring cup, whisk together the Cashew Sour Cream, vinegar, avocado oil, mustard, and onion powder. Pour this dressing over the cabbage. Mix well, so the cabbage is evenly and well coated with dressing. Taste the slaw and add salt as desired.

Toast the burger buns, if desired. Top each bottom half with 2 slices of the tempeh and a small heap of slaw, reserving extra slaw to serve alongside the sandwiches. Top the barbecue sandwiches with the bun tops. The tempeh slices will keep in an airtight container in the fridge for up to 5 days and can be frozen for up to 6 weeks. The slaw will keep in an airtight container in the fridge for up to 3 days.

BARBECUE TEMPEH

1 (8-ounce / 225g) block tempeh

¼ cup / 65g tomato paste

2 tablespoons water

2 tablespoons Bragg Liquid Aminos, soy sauce, or tamari

2 tablespoons avocado oil

2 tablespoons pure maple syrup

1 tablespoon apple cider vinegar

1 tablespoon molasses

1 teaspoon smoked paprika

½ teaspoon chili powder

SLAW

3 cups / 150g lightly packed shredded green cabbage

3 cups / 150g lightly packed shredded red cabbage

1 cup / 100g lightly packed shredded carrots

½ cup / 120ml Cashew Sour Cream (page 216) or store-bought vegan mayonnaise

1½ tablespoons apple cider vinegar

1 tablespoon avocado oil

1 tablespoon Dijon mustard

½ teaspoon onion powder

Salt

4 burger buns, split

Makes 4 servings

Grain: spelt bread
Green: arugula
Bean: white beans

———————

1 small kabocha squash, halved, seeded, and cut into ¼-inch / 6mm slices

2 red onions, thinly sliced

2 tablespoons avocado oil

Salt and freshly ground black pepper

1 tablespoon red or white balsamic vinegar

8 slices spelt bread, whole-wheat sandwich bread, or other sandwich bread

¾ cup / 85g White Bean Dip (page 220)

2 cups / 40g packed baby arugula

ROASTED KABOCHA SLICES, WHITE BEAN DIP, AND ARUGULA

There's a vegan cafe in New York City called Peacefood that serves some of the best sandwiches I've ever had. One of those sandwiches features kabocha squash, which I think is ingenious. Thin slices of this squash have the firm texture that works well as a sandwich stuffer. The Peacefood version has caramelized onions and cashew cheese. My tribute version features White Bean Dip, roasted red onions, and a handful of peppery arugula. It's one of my very favorite lunch sandwiches to eat in the fall and winter. If you don't have or can't find kabocha squash, try thinly sliced sweet potato rounds.

Preheat the oven to 400°F / 220°C. Line two sheet pans with aluminum foil or use two nonstick sheet pans.

Spread the squash slices on one prepared sheet pan and arrange in a single layer. Spread the red onion slices on the other prepared sheet pan. Drizzle 1 tablespoon of avocado oil over each sheet and give both squash and onion a generous sprinkle of salt and pepper. Use your hands to mix the vegetables on the sheets so they're coated with the oil and seasonings.

Place both sheet pans in the oven. Roast for 10 minutes, then stir the onions and flip the squash pieces over, ensuring that everything will cook evenly. Return the sheet pans to the oven. Roast the squash for another 5 to 15 minutes, until the slices are golden brown. Roast the onions for another 10 to 15 minutes, until they are soft and browning as well. Drizzle the onions with the vinegar and mix with a spoon or spatula to coat well.

Toast the bread slices, if you like. Spread 3 tablespoons of the White Bean Dip on each of four slices. Top each with one-fourth of the kabocha slices, add a layer of roasted onions, and sprinkle on ½ cup / 10g of arugula. Close the sandwiches with the remaining slices, then slice the sandwiches in half and serve. Roasted squash and onions will keep in an airtight container in the fridge for up to 5 days.

RED PEPPER HUMMUS AND ARUGULA
WITH ROASTED PORTOBELLO CAPS

Makes 4 servings

Grain: ciabatta rolls
Green: arugula
Bean: chickpeas

There's nothing quite like a big, round, juicy roasted portobello mushroom cap. It's savory, it's substantial, and it's not hard to understand why these mushrooms are so often described as "meaty"—and treated accordingly—in plant-based recipes. I happen to love a marinated and baked portobello mushroom cap in a sandwich, and this version, which also uses creamy red pepper hummus and peppery arugula, is my favorite.

Place the mushroom caps in a large rectangular storage container with a lid. In a small bowl or liquid measuring cup, whisk together the vinegar, avocado oil, soy sauce, maple syrup, Italian seasoning, and garlic. Pour this liquid marinade over the mushroom caps, then flip the tops around so you coat both tops and undersides of the mushrooms. Cover the container and place in the fridge for at least 4 hours and up to overnight.

Preheat the oven to 425°F / 220°C. Line a sheet pan with aluminum foil or parchment paper or use a nonstick sheet pan.

Remove the mushroom caps from their marinade (reserving the marinade), and transfer to the prepared sheet pan, tops up. Roast the caps for 25 to 35 minutes, flipping them once halfway through roasting, until they've reduced substantially in size and are browning.

Line a work surface with a few paper towels, then transfer the mushroom caps to the towels, allowing them to drain and dry a bit so they don't make your sandwiches soggy.

Place the arugula into a medium bowl and pour 2 tablespoons of the reserved marinade over it. Toss the arugula with the marinade.

Toast the rolls, if desired. Spread 3 tablespoons of the hummus on each of four slices. Top the slices with a roasted portobello cap and ½ cup of the arugula. Top each sandwich with a roll top, then cut the sandwiches in half and enjoy. The roasted portobello caps can be stored in an airtight container in the fridge for up to 5 days.

4 large fresh portobello mushroom caps, scrubbed and stemmed

⅓ cup / 80ml balsamic vinegar

¼ cup / 60ml avocado oil

1½ tablespoons soy sauce, tamari, or Bragg Liquid Aminos

1 tablespoon pure maple syrup or agave nectar

1 teaspoon dried Italian seasoning or dried oregano

2 garlic cloves, minced or finely grated

2 cups / 40g loosely packed fresh baby arugula

4 ciabatta rolls, or 4 (4-inch / 10cm) squares of vegan focaccia bread, sliced in half crosswise

¾ cup / 180ml Red Pepper Hummus (page 219)

Makes 4 servings

Grain: rye bread
Green: brussels sprouts
Bean: lentils

————————

1 tablespoon olive oil

10 ounces / 300g brussels sprouts, trimmed and thinly sliced lengthwise

Salt and freshly ground black pepper

8 slices rye or marbled rye sandwich bread

4 tablespoons / 60g store-bought onion jam or cranberry relish, or homemade cranberry sauce; or 4 tablespoons / 60g grainy mustard (optional)

4 thick slices Sweet Potato Lentil Loaf (page 174)

LENTIL LOAF SLICES WITH
SHAVED BRUSSELS SPROUTS

One of the reasons I make my Sweet Potato Lentil Loaf routinely is to have an excuse to make these hearty, homey sandwiches, which are faintly reminiscent of the popular Thanksgiving leftover sandwiches. When I make the loaf as an entrée, I serve it with roasted halved brussels sprouts. But for sandwiches, it's even easier to use sautéed shaved brussels sprouts. You can shave the sprouts yourself with a sharp chef's knife or use a food processor with the slicer attachment, but it's increasingly easy these days to find bags of shaved sprouts in grocery stores. Some optional spreads for this sandwich include store-bought onion jam, leftover cranberry sauce or store-bought cranberry relish, or—for a more savory take—some grainy mustard.

Heat the olive oil in a large skillet over medium heat. When the oil is shimmering, add the brussels sprouts. Sauté the sprouts, stirring frequently, for 5 to 7 minutes, until they are tender and just browning at the edges. Season the sprouts with salt and pepper as desired.

Toast the bread, if you like. Spread each of four slices with your spread of choice (if using), then top each with a slice of the lentil loaf. Follow with a heap of sautéed brussels sprouts. Close the sandwiches with the four remaining bread slices. Slice each sandwich in half and enjoy. Leftover lentil loaf slices will keep in an airtight container in the fridge for up to 5 days. They can be frozen for up to 6 weeks. Leftover sautéed sprouts will keep in an airtight container in the fridge for up to 4 days.

GREEN ONION AND BLACK BEAN TORTILLAS

Makes 2 servings

Grain: wheat tortilla
Green: green onions
Bean: black beans

Four bunches of green onions may sound like an incredible amount, but the thinly sliced stalks cook down to a heaping cup with only 5 minutes of sautéing. The green onions take on an almost creamy, caramelized texture, which makes them a perfect component for this easy, folded tortilla meal. The tortillas are pan-toasted and sliced, sort of like quesadillas, and the protein component of the filling is a spiced black bean mash. The recipe makes two large tortillas, but can easily be doubled if the prospect of chopping eight bunches of green onions doesn't scare you off.

Heat the avocado oil in a large skillet or frying pan over medium heat. Add the green onions and cook, stirring often, for 5 minutes, until very soft and reduced in volume greatly. Add the salt and red pepper flakes to taste.

Place the black beans in a medium bowl and add the lime juice, vinegar, cumin, and paprika. Use a potato masher or fork to partially mash the beans. They should be somewhat creamy, but also chunky for texture. Taste the beans; add salt and adjust the lime juice to taste.

Place one of the tortillas on a clean work surface. Spread half the black bean mixture on half the tortilla, in a semicircle shape. Cover this layer with half the green onions. Fold the uncovered tortilla over the filling. Repeat with the other tortilla.

Wipe the frying pan or skillet. Add a small amount of avocado oil to the pan or coat the pan with cooking oil spray. Heat the pan over medium-low heat. Add one of the folded tortillas and cook until lightly browned on each side, 2 to 3 minutes per side. Transfer to a cutting board and repeat with the other tortilla, then place the second toasted tortilla on the cutting board as well. Cut each tortilla into three wedges and serve. Both the black beans and the green onions can be prepared ahead of time and stored in airtight containers in the fridge for up to 4 days.

4 teaspoons avocado oil, plus more as needed

4 bunches green onions, bottoms and tips trimmed, stems sliced thinly crosswise

¼ teaspoon salt, or more as needed

Red pepper flakes

1½ cups / 240g cooked black beans, or 1 (15-ounce / 425g) can black beans, drained

1½ tablespoons freshly squeezed lime juice, or more as needed

1 teaspoon red or white balsamic vinegar

½ teaspoon ground cumin

¼ teaspoon smoked paprika

2 burrito-sized (10-inch / 25cm) wheat tortillas

There was a time when I felt exasperated by reader requests for one-pot recipes. It seemed limiting to me to cook with only one pot or pan, and I thought, "If more dishes make a better recipe, who cares?"

That was then, and this is now. These days, I care! A multi-step recipe can quickly create a sink stuffed with dirty dishes. The prospect of a heavy cleanup can be the final straw that makes a tired person open a food take-out app.

This chapter is designed with that tired person—often me—in mind. I can't promise all the recipes fit neatly into the "one pot" category, but that's the energy that I'm going for. Some recipes require boiling pasta in one pot while you simmer your beans and greens in another. For a few of them, you'll need to blend or whisk a sauce while letting other ingredients simmer on the stovetop. In the case of the Cornbread Muffins, Smoky Black-Eyed Peas, and Collard Greens (page 150), you'll bake some simple cornmeal muffins—the grain—while you prepare a hearty bean, greens, and sweet potato soup.

Nonetheless, these are cohesive, one-and-done meals that come together entirely or primarily on the stovetop. There's an emphasis on soups and pasta dishes, two of my favorite categories of food. But there's also a sweet and savory stir-fry of yuba and fresh tomatoes (see page 132), a gentle porridge of split peas and basmati rice (see page 152), and a dish of braised lentils and mushrooms (see page 138) that reminds me a little of beef bourguignon, though I doubt Julia would agree.

Meals of bowls and salads, with their many separate components, require strategic planning. In contrast, these stovetop meals can be more spontaneous. They can be go-to options for weeknight dinners or meals to pull together when friends come over on short notice. I'm a planner by nature, but these recipes have taught me how to flow.

STOVETOP MEALS

GIGANTES WITH KALE AND ORZO

Makes 4 to 6 servings

Grain: orzo

Green: kale, parsley, oregano

Bean: butter beans

---

2 tablespoons olive oil

1 small white or yellow onion, chopped

2 small celery stalks, chopped

2 small carrots, scrubbed or peeled and chopped

4 garlic cloves, minced

1 (28-ounce / 800g) can whole peeled tomatoes, with juices

3 cups / 480g cooked butter beans, or 2 (15-ounce / 425g) cans butter beans, drained and rinsed

1 cup / 225g orzo

1½ cups / 360ml vegetable broth

1 small bunch Tuscan kale, stemmed, leaves torn into pieces (about 4 cups / 135g)

1 cup / 30g chopped fresh parsley

1 tablespoon chopped fresh oregano

Salt

Red pepper flakes

4 tablespoons / 30g Cheesy Topping (page 209)

Gigantes plaki, or baked giant beans, is the name of a beloved Greek dish of large, tender white beans baked in a tomato sauce with herbs. This is a stovetop version of that dish, which transforms it from a mezze into a full meal with the addition of orzo and kale. Traditionally, the recipe is made with fasolia gigantes, a cultivar of runner beans that has a protected food designation in Greece. Americanized versions of the recipe call for butter beans, which are the same as mature lima beans. If you can't find canned butter beans, cannellini beans will work well.

Heat the olive oil in a large, deep skillet (with a lid) over medium heat. Add the onion, celery, and carrots and cook for 5 to 7 minutes, stirring occasionally, until the vegetables are tender and the onion is translucent. Add the garlic. Continue to cook, stirring constantly, for 1 more minute, until the garlic is fragrant.

Add the tomatoes to the skillet. Using the back of a spoon, gently crush the tomatoes (careful, they'll spatter!). Add the beans, orzo, and broth. Bring the mixture to a vigorous simmer, then reduce the heat to low. Cover and simmer for 10 to 12 minutes, until the orzo is cooked al dente, stirring a few times during cooking.

Uncover the skillet, give it a stir, then pile the kale on top of the orzo mixture. Recover and steam the kale for another 5 minutes, until the greens are tender.

Add the parsley and oregano to the skillet, then stir everything well, so the steamed kale and herbs are mixed into the orzo and bean mixture. Taste and add salt and red pepper flakes as needed.

Divide the gigantes and kale among serving bowls and top each portion with as much Cheesy Topping as you like. Serve at once. The beans, kale, and sauce can be stored in an airtight container, or place the components into individual containers, and kept for up to 5 days in the fridge.

BASMATI RICE, CHICKPEAS, AND MASALA GREEN BEANS
WITH EGGPLANT

Makes 4 servings

Grain: basmati rice
Green: green beans
Bean: chickpeas

Garam masala is a spice blend that often includes cinnamon, coriander, cumin, black peppercorns, and bay leaves. It can have sweet, astringent, and spicy notes depending on the blend, and it's a great pantry item to keep at home. In this recipe, garam masala is the primary seasoning for tender, sautéed eggplant and green beans. The best way to complete this flavorful meal is to top it with a big squeeze of lemon and some Cashew Sour Cream.

Place the eggplant cubes in a colander and salt generously. Allow the eggplant to sit for 20 minutes; it will appear to "sweat" somewhat. Use tea towels or paper towels to firmly pat it dry.

While the eggplant is salting, rinse the rice under cold running water until the water runs clear. Drain the rice and add to a medium pot along with the water. Bring the water to a boil, turn the heat to low, cover the pot, and simmer the rice for 13 minutes. Remove the rice from the heat. Allow it to stand for 5 minutes before fluffing it lightly with a spoon or rice paddle. Re-cover the rice and set it aside.

Heat the avocado oil in a heavy-bottomed large pot over medium heat. When the oil is shimmering, add the onion. Sauté for 4 to 5 minutes, until becoming translucent. Add the garlic, ginger, garam masala, turmeric, and ¼ teaspoon of salt and continue to sauté for another minute, until the aromatics and spices are fragrant.

Add the salted eggplant to the pot. Sauté the eggplant, stirring occasionally, for 8 to 10 minutes, until the eggplant starts to tenderize and some of the skin is slightly browning. Add the chickpeas, tomatoes, and green beans to the pot, stir the ingredients, and bring everything to a gentle simmer. Cover the pot, turn the heat to low, and simmer the ingredients for 10 to 15 minutes, until the eggplant is very tender. Taste the mixture and add red pepper flakes for heat, if desired.

Divide the rice among four bowls and top each with one-fourth of the eggplant mixture. Add the cilantro or Cashew Sour Cream (if using). The rice can be stored in an airtight container in the fridge for up to 4 days and the eggplant mixture for up to 5 days. The eggplant mixture can also be frozen for up to 6 weeks.

2 graffiti eggplants or 1 large globe eggplant, trimmed and cut into 1-inch / 2.5cm cubes (about 1 pound / 455g)

Salt

1 cup / 180g white basmati rice

1½ cups / 360ml water

2 tablespoons avocado oil

1 white or yellow onion, chopped

3 garlic cloves, minced

2 teaspoons finely grated or minced fresh ginger

2 teaspoons garam masala (or 1 teaspoon cumin, ½ teaspoon allspice, ½ teaspoon cinnamon, and ⅛ teaspoon freshly ground black pepper)

½ teaspoon ground turmeric

1½ cups / 240g cooked chickpeas, or 1 (15-ounce / 425g) can chickpeas, drained

1 (14.5-ounce / 415g) can diced tomatoes, with juices

12 ounces / 340g fresh green beans, trimmed and cut into 2-inch / 5cm pieces

Red pepper flakes (optional)

Chopped fresh cilantro, Cashew Sour Cream (page 216), or both, for topping (optional)

Makes 4 servings

Grain: lo mein noodles
Green: baby bok choy
Bean: TVP

⅔ cup / 65g texturized vegetable protein (TVP)

3 cups / 720ml water

1 tablespoon and 2 teaspoons avocado oil, divided

3 tablespoons soy sauce

1 to 2 tablespoons chili crisp

2 tablespoons unseasoned rice vinegar

2 tablespoons tahini

1 tablespoon pure maple syrup or agave nectar

2 garlic cloves, finely minced or grated

¼ teaspoon Chinese five-spice powder

¼ cup / 60ml vegetable broth or vegan chicken-style broth

4 heads baby bok choy, quartered lengthwise

4 green onions, white and green parts, thinly sliced crosswise

8 ounces / 225g lo mein or udon noodles

NOODLES WITH SPICY SOY PROTEIN AND BABY BOK CHOY

Many assume that plant-based meats are a contemporary invention, but soy and wheat proteins have been used to make "mock meats" in parts of Asia for centuries. In this recipe, sautéed TVP and green onions are heated with a spicy sauce and then piled on top of lo mein noodles and bok choy. I love the first swirl of noodles on my fork after I've mixed the ingredients together!

Place the TVP in a medium bowl. Bring the water to a boil in a medium saucepan or microwave it for 4 to 5 minutes in a heatproof liquid measuring cup, then pour the hot water over the TVP. Allow the TVP to soak up the liquid for 10 minutes, then drain it through a fine-mesh strainer or colander. Use the bottom of the bowl to press down on the TVP a bit as it drains, helping to remove as much moisture as possible. Set aside.

In a small bowl or a liquid measuring cup, whisk together 1 tablespoon of the avocado oil, the soy sauce, chili crisp (to your preferred level of heat), rice vinegar, tahini, maple syrup, garlic, five-spice powder, and broth.

Put a few inches of water in a medium pot and fit the pot with a steamer attachment. Bring the water to a simmer, then steam the bok choy for 5 to 7 minutes, until very tender. Set the bok choy aside and remove the steamer attachment from the pot. Fill the pot with fresh water and bring it to a boil.

Heat the remaining 2 teaspoons avocado oil in a large, deep skillet or frying pan over medium heat. Add the green onions and cook for 1 minute, stirring constantly. Add the TVP and continue cooking, stirring often, for 4 to 5 minutes, until the green onions are fragrant and the TVP is just browning. Stir in the sauce and continue heating and stirring. Once the sauce and TVP mixture is hot, in 2 to 3 minutes, remove the skillet from the heat.

When the water in the pot is boiling, add the noodles. Cook, drain, and rinse according to package instructions.

Divide the noodles and bok choy among four bowls, then top each portion with one-fourth of the TVP and sauce. Enjoy. The TVP and its sauce can be prepared ahead of time and stored in an airtight container in the fridge for up to 5 days. It can also be frozen for up to 6 weeks.

QUINOA, BABY LIMA BEANS, AND GREEN BEANS

Makes 4 servings

Grain: quinoa
Green: green beans, basil
Bean: baby lima beans

———————

This dish is inspired by succotash, a bean and corn stew that Indigenous peoples of North America introduced to colonizers in the seventeenth century. Today, succotash can include a variety of legumes and vegetables; my favorite version has cherry tomatoes, sweet corn, onion, green beans, and baby lima beans. I usually buy baby lima beans frozen, but if you can't find a bag of those, usually there are canned baby limas on grocery store shelves. The grain here is a fluffy bed of quinoa, but I also like to serve this with homemade corn muffins (see page 150).

1 cup / 180g white or red quinoa

1¾ cups / 415ml water

2 tablespoons avocado oil

1 small white or yellow onion, chopped

12 ounces / 340g cherry tomatoes

2¼ cups / 290g fresh or frozen corn kernels, or 1 (12 ounce / 340g) bag frozen kernels or kernels from 4 ears of corn

12 ounces / 340g fresh green beans, trimmed and cut into 2-inch / 5cm pieces

1½ cups / 255g baby lima beans, frozen and thawed or canned

½ teaspoon salt, or more as needed

1½ tablespoons freshly squeezed lemon juice, or more as needed

½ cup / 20g chopped fresh basil

Freshly ground black pepper

Rinse the quinoa in a fine-mesh strainer. Add the quinoa and water to a medium pot over medium-high heat. Bring the quinoa and water to a boil, cover, and turn the heat to low. Simmer for 13 minutes, covered, then remove the pot from the heat. Allow the quinoa to stand for 5 minutes, then fluff it with a fork. Re-cover and set aside.

Heat the avocado oil in a large, deep skillet (with a lid) over medium heat. When the oil is shimmering, add the onion. Sauté the onion, stirring frequently, for 4 minutes, until just translucent. Add the tomatoes and cover the skillet. Cook for 7 to 8 minutes, stirring occasionally, until the tomatoes have burst and are juicy.

Stir in the corn, green beans, and baby limas. Cover the skillet again and simmer for 5 to 7 minutes, stirring occasionally, until the green beans and limas are tender and the corn is both tender and sweet. Stir in the salt, lemon juice, and basil. Taste the mixture. Add pepper to taste and adjust the salt and lemon juice to your liking.

Divide the quinoa among four serving plates and top each portion with one-fourth of the bean and corn mixture. Both the cooked quinoa and the beans and vegetables will keep in an airtight container in the fridge for up to 5 days.

Makes 4 servings

Grain: orecchiette
Green: broccoli rabe
Bean: tempeh

---

8 ounces / 225g orecchiette (or other medium pasta)

1¾ cups / 415ml vegetable broth or vegan no-chicken broth

8 ounces / 225g tempeh, crumbled

1 teaspoon dried parsley

1 teaspoon dried oregano

⅛ teaspoon smoked paprika

½ teaspoon fennel seeds, crushed lightly with the back of a spoon

Heaping ¼ teaspoon garlic powder

2 tablespoons olive oil

3 garlic cloves, minced

1 bunch broccoli rabe, ends trimmed, remainder roughly chopped (about 340g)

1 tablespoon freshly squeezed lemon juice, or more as needed

½ teaspoon salt, or more as needed

5 tablespoons / 40g Cheesy Topping (page 209) or store-bought vegan parmesan cheese

Red pepper flakes

ORECCHIETTE WITH CRUMBLED TEMPEH AND BROCCOLI RABE

Pasta with sausage and broccoli is a hearty Italian classic. This is my plant-based expression of the recipe, which uses savory crumbled tempeh in place of meat. I also opt to use broccoli rabe, which is one of my favorite leafy greens. Broccoli rabe can be bitter and is an acquired taste, but I think it takes on a little sweetness through cooking. If you can't locate broccoli rabe, feel free to substitute broccoli florets instead.

Bring a large pot of salted water to a boil over high heat. Add the pasta and cook until al dente according to package instructions. Drain the pasta in a colander and reserve 1 cup of the cooking water.

In a large, deep skillet, combine the broth, tempeh, parsley, oregano, paprika, fennel seeds, and garlic powder. Bring the broth to a vigorous simmer over medium-high heat and add the tempeh to the skillet. Turn the heat to medium low and simmer the tempeh, uncovered, for 12 to 15 minutes, until all the broth has been absorbed or evaporated and the tempeh starts browning. Be sure to stir it every few minutes toward the end of cooking. Cover and set aside.

Add the olive oil to the pot used to cook the pasta and warm over medium-low heat. Add the garlic and cook the garlic for 30 seconds, stirring constantly. Add the broccoli rabe and stir. Cover and allow the greens to steam for 2 minutes. Uncover the greens and continue cooking, stirring frequently, for an additional 2 to 4 minutes, until the greens are tender but bright in color and with some bite.

Add the pasta to the greens along with two-thirds of the reserved cooking water, the lemon juice, salt, and Cheesy Topping. Simmer, stirring frequently, for 2 to 3 minutes, until the water has been absorbed. Stir in the tempeh mixture, along with the remaining cooking water, or as much as is needed for the pasta to loosen and glisten but not so much as to be liquidy. Cook for another minute, until the pasta is glistening and hot throughout.

Taste the pasta and add additional salt, lemon juice, and some red pepper flakes to taste. Serve at once. The cooked pasta mixture can be stored in an airtight container in the fridge for up to 3 days.

RED LENTIL CARROT SOUP
WITH PEARL COUSCOUS

Makes 4 servings

Grain: pearl couscous
Green: leafy green
Bean: red lentils

———————

2 tablespoons olive oil

1 white onion, diced

1 large or 2 small celery stalks, diced

1½ pounds / 680g carrots, scrubbed or peeled, trimmed, and finely chopped

2 tablespoons tomato paste

2 garlic cloves, minced

1 teaspoon ground cumin

¾ teaspoon ground coriander

1 teaspoon salt

1 cup / 200g dried red lentils

2 quarts / 1.9L vegetable broth

½ cup / 100g pearl couscous

1 small bunch kale, chard, turnip greens, beet greens, or spinach, stemmed and roughly chopped

1½ tablespoons freshly squeezed lemon juice

Red pepper flakes

Chopped fresh parsley, for serving (optional)

There's something about the combination of red lentils and carrots that I love, whether it's their similarity in color or the way their sweet and earthy flavors work together. This stew highlights both ingredients, and it introduces pearl couscous for a fun texture contrast. I recommend chopping the carrots more finely than you might usually, so some of them seem to melt into the soup along with the lentils. This creates a lovely, thick consistency without any need for a blender. For this recipe, as with some of the other soups and stews in this book, you can use any leafy green you have on hand: kale, chard, spinach, beet greens, and turnip greens are all good additions.

Heat the olive oil in a heavy-bottomed large pot over medium heat. Add the onion, celery, and carrots. Cook the vegetables, stirring occasionally, for 8 to 10 minutes, until the carrots have softened and the onion is translucent. Stir in the tomato paste, garlic, cumin, coriander, and salt, and cook, stirring constantly, for 1 more minute.

Add the red lentils and broth to the pot. Bring the mixture to a boil, then reduce the heat to low. Cover and simmer the soup for 20 minutes, until the lentils are completely softened. Add the couscous and greens to the soup, then re-cover and simmer for 10 more minutes, until the couscous and greens are both tender.

Add the lemon juice to the soup and red pepper flakes to taste. Serve, garnished with fresh parsley (if using). The soup can be stored in an airtight container in the fridge for up to 1 week and frozen for up to 6 weeks.

Makes 4 servings

Grain: long-grain white rice
Green: green onions, spinach
Bean: yuba

_____

1 cup / 180g long-grain white rice, rinsed

1½ cups / 360ml and ¼ cup / 60ml water, divided

1 tablespoon avocado oil

4 green onions, whites and green tops, thinly sliced crosswise

3 large ripe tomatoes, seeded and chopped, or 1 (28-ounce / 800g) can whole peeled tomatoes, drained and roughly chopped

3 garlic cloves, minced

1 tablespoon white miso

1½ tablespoons soy sauce

5 ounces / 140g yuba, fresh or thawed, cut into 1½-inch / 4cm strips

4 cups / 80g lightly packed baby spinach

YUBA AND TOMATO STIR-FRY

Yuba, or tofu skin, is the thin and rubbery sheets that form when soy milk is coagulated into blocks of soy curd (aka tofu). While it may be a by-product of the tofu-making process, yuba has its own culinary personality: its bouncy, chewy layers are great in stir-fries, soups, and salads. One of the most intriguing yuba preparations I've come across is a stir-fry of yuba and tomatoes, where yuba is reminiscent of egg. I like to add a miso slurry to my version, which infuses the dish with a savory, buttery quality, and I add both green onions and spinach for a green component. My favorite way to serve this stir-fry is over a bed of simple white rice, but I also love to pile it onto sourdough or white sandwich bread.

Yuba comes in sheets and is sold in three different forms: dried, frozen, and fresh. Dried yuba requires rehydration in hot water before using, just like TVP or soy curls. Be sure to drain and pat the sheets dry before you cook with them, so they can absorb sauce and seasoning. Frozen yuba is found in the frozen section of many Asian grocers. It can be thawed overnight in the fridge before use. Fresh yuba can be the most difficult type to find, but it's conveniently ready to use. My favorite fresh yuba is made by Hodo Foods, a California brand that also makes excellent tofu.

In a medium pot over medium-high heat, add the rice and the 1½ cups / 360ml water. Bring the water to a simmer, then turn the heat to low. Cover the pot and simmer the rice for 12 minutes. Remove the pot from the heat and allow the rice to steam for another 10 minutes, then fluff it gently with a fork. Re-cover and set aside.

In a large, deep skillet, heat the avocado oil over medium heat. Add the green onions and tomatoes and sauté, stirring frequently, for 3 minutes, until the tomatoes release their juices. Add the garlic and turn the heat to low. Continue sautéing for another 2 to 3 minutes, until the mixture turns saucy and the garlic is fragrant.

In a small bowl, mix the miso with the ¼ cup / 60ml water to make a slurry. Add the slurry and the soy sauce to the skillet and stir to combine. Add the yuba and bring the mixture to a simmer again. Add the spinach to the skillet in handfuls, stirring as you do, then simmer

for another 2 to 3 minutes, until the spinach is wilted and the yuba seems to have absorbed some of the savory, sweet juices.

To serve, divide the rice among four plates or bowls and top each portion with one-fourth of the stir-fry. The rice can be stored in an airtight container in the fridge for up to 3 days, and the yuba and tomato stir-fry can be stored for up to 5 days.

WHEAT BERRY, BEET, AND LENTIL SOUP WITH SAUERKRAUT

Makes 4 servings

Grain: wheat berries
Green: sauerkraut
(green cabbage)
Bean: lentils

———————

1 tablespoon olive oil

2 leeks, white parts only, trimmed, sliced crosswise into ½-inch / 1.3cm pieces, cleaned thoroughly

2 celery stalks, chopped

4 garlic cloves, minced

8 cups / 1.9L water, plus more as needed

1 cup / 160g wheat berries

½ cup / 90g dried lentils du Puy

3 red beets, scrubbed and shredded

½ teaspoon salt, or more as needed

1½ cups / 180g caraway-flavored sauerkraut (or regular)

Freshly ground black pepper

1 cup / 240ml Cashew Sour Cream (page 216), for serving (optional)

Chopped fresh dill, for serving (optional)

Beets, caraway-studded sauerkraut, and wheat berries: this one-pot soup captures a few of the ingredients I grew up loving in New York City, where rye bread, borscht, and Reuben sandwiches are all deli mainstays. The sweet and earthy flavors of beets and lentils are so nicely balanced with the great big scoop of the caraway sauerkraut that is added to the soup at the end of its simmering time. (If you can't find the caraway sauerkraut, use regular sauerkraut.) Top the soup with a dollop of Cashew Sour Cream and some dill sprigs, and serve it with rye toast points, if you like.

In a heavy-bottomed large pot, heat the olive oil over medium heat. Add the leeks and celery and sauté, stirring often, for 5 to 7 minutes, until the leeks and celery are tender. Stir in the garlic and continue cooking for 1 more minute, stirring constantly, until the garlic is fragrant.

Add the water and wheat berries to the pot. Bring the mixture to a boil, cover, and turn the heat to low. Simmer for 30 minutes. Add the lentils and beets, turn the heat to high, and return the mixture to a boil. Once again, turn the heat to low, cover, and continue simmering for another 30 to 40 minutes, until the wheat berries and lentils are both tender. Stir in the salt and sauerkraut, then simmer the soup for 5 more minutes to help the flavors meld. If the soup has become too thick, add up to an additional 2 cups / 480ml water at this time. Taste the soup, adjust the salt, and add pepper as needed.

Divide the soup among four bowls. Top each portion with a few tablespoons of the Cashew Sour Cream and some fresh dill (if using). Serve. The soup can be kept in an airtight container in the fridge for up to 1 week.

Makes 6 servings

Grain: vermicelli
Green: celery stalks,
celery leaves, cilantro
Bean: lentils, chickpeas

———————

2 tablespoons olive oil

1 yellow or white onion, chopped

2 carrots, peeled and chopped

2 celery stalks, chopped

½ cup / 10g packed celery leaves, roughly chopped

4 garlic cloves, minced

2 tablespoons tomato paste

1 teaspoon ground turmeric

1 teaspoon ground cumin

½ teaspoon ground cinnamon

½ teaspoon ground ginger

½ teaspoon fine sea salt

¾ cup / 150g dried green or brown lentils

1 (28-ounce / 800g) can crushed tomatoes, with their juices

8 cups / 1.9L vegetable broth

1½ cups / 240g cooked chickpeas, or 1 (15-ounce / 425g) can chickpeas, drained and rinsed

½ cup / 10g lightly packed chopped fresh cilantro (or parsley, if you don't care for cilantro)

½ cup / 60g broken vermicelli wheat noodles (in about 1-inch / 2.5cm pieces), broken spaghetti, or fideos

2 tablespoons unbleached all-purpose flour

Freshly squeezed lime juice, for serving

Red pepper flakes, for serving

Cashew Sour Cream (page 216), for serving (optional)

BROKEN VERMICELLI AND LENTIL CHICKPEA STEW WITH HERBS

This nourishing stew is inspired by harira, a soup that's popular in Morocco and Algeria as a means of breaking the fast during Ramadan. Half the greens in this recipe are celery leaves, an often-discarded part of the stalks that here are chopped and included in the soup base. I'll confess that celery isn't my favorite vegetable, but I love what the leaves do in this instance; they add an herbal, almost lemony quality to the soup. Broken noodles—vermicelli wheat noodles or spaghetti, or fideos—help to thicken this dish, which can be a meal unto itself.

In a heavy-bottomed large pot, heat the olive oil over medium heat. When the oil is shimmering, add the onion, carrots, celery, and celery leaves. Sauté the vegetables, stirring frequently, for 6 to 8 minutes, until the onion is translucent and the carrots are tender. Add the garlic, tomato paste, turmeric, cumin, cinnamon, ginger, and salt to the pot. Continue sautéing this mixture, stirring constantly, for 1 to 2 minutes, until the tomato paste is fully combined with the vegetables and the garlic is fragrant.

Add the lentils, tomatoes, and broth to the pot. Cover the pot, turn the heat to high, and bring the mixture to a boil. Turn the heat to low, cover again, and simmer the ingredients for 15 minutes.

Add the chickpeas, cilantro, and vermicelli pieces to the pot. Cover and simmer for another 8 to 10 minutes, until the lentils are fully cooked and the noodles are tender.

Place the flour in a small bowl and add ¼ cup / 60ml of the soup broth. Stir to create a slurry, then pour this mixture back into the soup. Stir the soup well, then allow it to simmer for 5 additional minutes, uncovered, until it's thickened. Add the lime juice and red pepper flakes to taste.

Divide the soup among six bowls and serve. If desired, add a spoonful of Cashew Sour Cream to each bowl. The soup will keep in an airtight container in the fridge for up to 6 days and can be frozen for up to 6 weeks.

Makes 6 servings

Grain: farro

Green: kale

Bean: lentils

_____

2 tablespoons and
1 tablespoon olive oil,
divided

2 pounds / 900g mixed
fresh mushrooms (such as
portobello, cremini, baby
bella, shiitake, and button),
sliced

Salt

2 leeks, white parts only,
trimmed, sliced crosswise
into ½-inch / 1.3cm pieces,
cleaned thoroughly

2 carrots, trimmed, scrubbed,
and chopped

2 garlic cloves, minced

2 tablespoons tomato paste

½ teaspoon dried oregano

½ teaspoon dried thyme

1 cup / 240ml medium- or
full-bodied dry red wine

2 tablespoons all-purpose
flour

3 cups / 720ml vegan beef-
style broth or vegetable broth

¾ cup / 150g dried lentils
du Puy

1 cup / 130g thawed frozen
pearl onions

4 cups / 60g loosely packed
chopped curly or Tuscan
kale (or collard greens or
chard), or 4 cups / 80g lightly
packed fresh baby spinach
leaves

Freshly ground black pepper

1½ cups / 270g pearled farro

RED WINE BRAISED MUSHROOMS AND FRENCH LENTILS WITH FARRO

While totally unlike beef bourguignon in its simplicity (and its omission of animal protein), this dish nonetheless captures some of the qualities of that classic. First, there's the flavor profile: red wine, herbs, pearl onions, and garlic. Then, there's the wintery heartiness: mushrooms and lentils for meaty texture. You can serve this dish over pasta, toast, or polenta, but my favorite option is to pile it on top of some farro. The grain's nutty flavor and chewy texture can stand up to the earthy intensity of the stew.

In a heavy-bottomed large pot, heat the 2 tablespoons olive oil over medium-high heat. Add the mushrooms and a pinch of salt. Allow the mushrooms to cook without stirring for 4 to 5 minutes, until they've released their juices. Stir the mushrooms and sauté for another 6 to 8 minutes, stirring occasionally, until the mushrooms are tender and lightly browning. Transfer the mushrooms to a plate and set aside.

Add the remaining tablespoon oil to the pot set over medium heat. Add the leeks and carrots and sauté for 6 to 8 minutes, stirring often, until the leeks are translucent and the carrots are tender. Stir in the garlic, tomato paste, oregano, and thyme. Cook, stirring constantly, for 1 more minute, until the garlic is fragrant.

Add the wine to the pot and turn the heat to high. Allow the wine to simmer vigorously for 5 minutes, until reduced by half. Sprinkle the flour over the ingredients and stir well to combine, making sure there are no spots of clumped flour.

Add the mushrooms back to the pot and stir. Pour in 1 cup / 240ml of the broth to the pot in a thin stream, stirring as you go. Add the remaining broth and the lentils. Bring the mixture to a boil, then turn the heat to low. Cover the pot and simmer for 30 minutes.

Add the pearl onions and kale and simmer for an additional 15 minutes, until the lentils, onions, and kale are tender and the mixture resembles a thick stew. Taste the stew and adjust the salt and add freshly ground black pepper as needed.

Meanwhile, bring a medium pot of water to a boil. Add the farro. Boil, uncovered, like pasta, for 30 minutes, until the farro is tender yet still

retains its chewiness. Drain the farro, then return it to the pot. Cover the farro and allow it to rest until the mushrooms and lentils are ready.

Divide the farro among six plates or shallow bowls. Top each portion with some of the mushroom and lentil mixture. Serve. The cooked farro and mushroom and lentil stew can each be stored in airtight containers in the fridge for up to 6 days.

Grain: radiatori pasta
Green: zucchini
Bean: cannellini beans

---

8 ounces / 225g radiatori pasta

2 tablespoons olive oil

1 large zucchini, trimmed, halved lengthwise, and cut crosswise into ½-inch / 1.3cm pieces

12 ounces / 340g ripe Sungold or cherry tomatoes

3 garlic cloves, minced

1½ cups / 280g cooked cannellini beans, or 1 (14.5-ounce/ 415g) can cannellini beans, drained

Salt and freshly ground black pepper

1 to 2 tablespoons freshly squeezed lemon juice

¼ cup / 10g chopped fresh basil (optional)

2 tablespoons Cheesy Topping (page 209) or store-bought vegan parmesan cheese, plus extra for serving (optional)

RADIATORI, CANNELLINI BEANS, AND ZUCCHINI WITH BURST SUNGOLD TOMATOES

When Sungold tomatoes and zucchini pieces are pan-simmered for just under 10 minutes, the tomatoes burst and the zucchini becomes almost meltingly tender. As a result, these two ingredients turn into a beautiful, light, and effortless plant-based sauce for pasta and beans. I use cannellini beans in the recipe, and I mash them gently to help contribute to that saucy effect. Radiatori, with their pronounced ridges, are a great vehicle for soaking up the summery goodness, but any medium pasta shape that holds sauce well will work here.

Bring a large pot of salted water to a boil. Add the pasta and cook according to package instructions, until your liking. Drain the pasta in a colander and reserve 1 cup of the cooking water.

Heat the olive oil in a large, deep skillet over medium-high heat. When the oil is shimmering, add the zucchini and tomatoes. Stir the ingredients, then cover the pot and cook for 5 minutes. Give the pot a stir and continue cooking for another 3 to 5 minutes, until the tomatoes have burst. Add the garlic and cook for 30 seconds, until the garlic becomes quite fragrant, stirring constantly,

Turn the heat to low and add in the cannellini beans, along with ¼ cup / 60ml of the reserved cooking water. Stir the ingredients and cover the skillet. Simmer for 5 minutes, until the beans are hot and the tomatoes have become truly saucy. If you like, mash the beans a little with the back of a spoon to create an even more saucy effect in the pasta. Be sure to leave some of the beans whole for texture.

Add the pasta, ¼ teaspoon of salt, and ½ cup / 120ml of the cooking water to the skillet. Stir everything together, cover again, and simmer the pasta for 3 to 5 minutes, until the pasta is hot and seems to be soaking up the sauce. Taste the pasta. Stir in the lemon juice as desired and add salt and pepper to taste. Stir in the basil and Cheesy Topping (if using).

Divide the pasta and sauce among four plates or bowls, then serve with additional topping if desired. The pasta and sauce can be stored in an airtight container in the fridge for up to 3 days.

TURMERIC RICE, SOY CURLS, AND BROCCOLINI

Makes 4 servings

Grain: long-grain white rice
Green: broccolini
Bean: soy curls

_____

1 cup / 180g long-grain white rice or white basmati rice

1 tablespoon olive oil

1 white or yellow onion, diced

1 red bell pepper, diced

2 garlic cloves, minced

3 tablespoons / 50g tomato paste

¾ teaspoon ground turmeric

½ teaspoon smoked paprika

2 cups / 480ml vegetable broth

1 bunch broccolini, thicker bottom stems trimmed, remainder cut into 2- to 3-inch (5 to 7.5cm) pieces

1 batch (3 cups / 180g) Savory Soy Curls (page 213), or 3 cups / 340–675g store-bought vegan chick'n (weight varies depending on brand)

1 tablespoon freshly squeezed lime juice, or more as needed

Salt

1 cup / 240ml Red Pepper Sauce (page 214)

Imagine this: you make a batch of Savory Soy Curls and Red Pepper Sauce on a Sunday. Come Monday evening, no matter how gentle or chaotic the start to the week has been, you can have a hearty, colorful rice skillet supper on the table in half an hour. This has become a favorite weeknight meal for me, one that's as protein rich and satisfying as it is easy to make.

Place the rice into a bowl with enough water to submerge it by a few inches. Swish it around with your hands and let it soak for 10 minutes. Rinse the rice thoroughly under cold running water and drain well.

In a large, deep skillet, heat the olive oil over medium heat. When the oil is shimmering, add the onion and bell pepper. Sauté the vegetables for 3 to 5 minutes, stirring frequently, until the onion is just translucent. Add the garlic, tomato paste, turmeric, and paprika. Continue sautéing this mixture, stirring constantly, for 1 to 2 minutes, until the tomato paste is fully blended into the vegetables and the garlic is fragrant.

Add the rice to the skillet. Mix well with the other ingredients. Pour the broth into the skillet. Cover the skillet, turn the heat to high, and bring the broth to a boil. Turn the heat to low and simmer, covered, for 7 minutes.

Uncover the skillet and arrange the broccolini pieces on top of the rice. Re-cover and simmer for another 5 minutes, until the rice has completely absorbed the broth and the broccolini is tender and bright green. Add the soy curls and lime juice, and gently fold the ingredients together. Cover the skillet once more and continue simmering for 1 to 2 minutes, until the ingredients are warmed through. Taste and add additional lime juice and salt as needed, keeping in mind that the red pepper sauce will add flavor.

Divide the rice and soy curls among four plates. Top each portion with ¼ cup / 60ml of the red pepper sauce. Enjoy. The rice will keep for up to 4 days in an airtight container in the fridge, and it can be frozen for up to 6 weeks.

—————

1 pound / 450g dried green
split peas

8 cups / 1.9L vegetable broth
or vegan chicken-style broth

2 tablespoons olive oil

1 large white onion, diced

3 large carrots, trimmed
and diced

3 celery stalks, trimmed
and diced

¾ teaspoon smoked paprika

1 teaspoon dried thyme

½ teaspoon salt, or more
as needed

4 cups / 120g lightly packed
fresh baby spinach or
chopped mature spinach

Freshly ground black pepper

CROUTONS

½ loaf (1-pound / 450g)
country bread or sourdough
bread, cut or torn into
1-inch / 2.5cm pieces

¼ cup / 60ml olive oil

1 teaspoon garlic powder

½ teaspoon fine sea salt

¼ teaspoon freshly ground
black pepper

Cashew Sour Cream
(page 216; optional)

CREAMY SPLIT PEA SPINACH SOUP
WITH GARLICKY CROUTONS

This recipe is based on a traditional split pea soup, with smoked paprika supplying some of the flavor that ham might offer in an omnivorous version. The twist here is the addition of spinach, which is blended into the soup while it's hot. The result is a bright green, warming, nutritious mixture that's even better with a batch of crispy, rustic, homemade croutons—this recipe's grain. I love split peas, but I've learned that their cooking time can be unpredictable and sometimes long. I recommend soaking them overnight prior to cooking as an insurance policy! You can enjoy the soup as it is, or add creaminess with a swirled spoonful of Cashew Sour Cream.

The night before you prepare the soup, place the split peas in a large bowl and add enough water to cover them by several inches. Place the bowl in the fridge to soak overnight.

The following day, drain and rinse the split peas, then add them to a large pot, along with the broth. Bring the mixture to a boil over medium-high heat, then reduce the heat to low. Cover and simmer the soup for 1 hour, until the split peas are so tender that some of them are breaking apart.

Meanwhile, heat the olive oil in a heavy-bottomed large pot over medium heat. Add the onion, carrots, and celery. Sauté the vegetables, stirring occasionally, for 6 to 8 minutes, until the onion is translucent and the vegetables are soft. Stir in the paprika, thyme, and salt.

Transfer 4 cups / 950ml of the soup to a blender and add the spinach. Blend this mixture for a minute, until it's thick and smooth. Return the blended mixture to the pot and stir. If the soup is too thick for your liking, add a bit of water to loosen it. Taste the soup and adjust the salt and pepper as needed. Cover and set aside.

Make the croutons. Preheat the oven to 375°F / 190°C.

Spread the bread cubes on a large sheet pan. Drizzle with the olive oil, then sprinkle with the garlic powder, salt, and pepper. Use your hands to mix the croutons on the sheet, coating them well with the seasonings. Place the sheet pan in the oven and bake the croutons for 10 minutes. Stir the croutons, then bake for another 5 to 10 minutes, until browning and crispy.

To serve, divide the soup among six bowls. Stir a spoonful of Cashew Sour Cream (if using) into each bowl. Top the bowls with a generous handful of the croutons and enjoy. The soup can be stored in an airtight container in the fridge for up to 6 days and can be frozen for up to 6 weeks. The croutons can be stored in an airtight container in the fridge for up to 4 days and reheated in a 350° / 175°C oven for 10 minutes to regain their crispy texture.

PASTA, KIDNEY BEAN, AND KALE STEW

Makes 4 to 6 servings

Grain: short pasta
Green: green beans, kale
Bean: cannellini beans

———————

I grew up eating canned minestrone, which wasn't bad, but it certainly wasn't as soul-satisfying as this homemade tribute to the rustic Tuscan vegetable-and-pasta stew. You can use any short pasta shape you like here; I like to use mezze rigatoni, medium or small shells, elbows, or orecchiette. Likewise, you have a choice of what beans to use. I've made the soup successfully with red kidney beans, cannellini beans, chickpeas, navy beans, pinto beans, and black-eyed peas. There are 2 tablespoons of Cheesy Topping stirred into the soup at the end, but I recommend a generous spoonful on top for serving, too.

In a heavy-bottomed large pot, heat the olive oil over medium heat. Add the onion, celery, and carrots. Cook the vegetables, stirring occasionally, for 6 to 8 minutes, until the onion is translucent and the vegetables are tender. Add the garlic and tomato paste to the pot. Stir well, distributing the paste evenly over the diced vegetables. Cook for 1 to 2 minutes, stirring often, until the garlic is fragrant.

Add the diced tomatoes, broth, kidney beans, water, and pasta to the pot. Raise the heat and bring this mixture to a boil. Reduce the heat to low, cover, and simmer for 10 minutes, until the pasta has become plump but is still al dente. Add the green beans and kale to the pot and cover. Simmer for another 5 to 8 minutes, until the kale is tender. Stir in the Cheesy Topping. If the soup is too thick for your liking, stir in up to an additional 1 cup / 240ml water.

Taste the soup and add salt and pepper to taste. Serve or store in an airtight container in the fridge for up to 5 days. You can freeze the soup for up to 2 weeks.

Ingredients

2 tablespoons olive oil

1 white or yellow onion, diced

2 celery stalks, diced

3 carrots, trimmed and diced

4 garlic cloves, minced

¼ cup / 65g tomato paste

1 (28-ounce / 800g) can diced regular or petite tomatoes, with juices

4 cups / 950ml vegetable broth

1½ cups / 280g cooked kidney or cannellini beans, or 1 (14.5-ounce / 415g) can beans, drained and rinsed

2 cups / 480ml water, or more as needed

1½ cups / 115g short pasta shape of choice

8 ounces / 225g fresh green beans, trimmed and cut into 2-inch / 5cm pieces

1 bunch Tuscan kale, thick bottom stems removed, remainder sliced crosswise into ½-inch / 1.3cm ribbons

2 heaping tablespoons Cheesy Topping (page 209), plus more for serving

Salt and freshly ground black pepper

Makes 4 servings

Grain: couscous
Green: zucchini, green peas
Bean: chickpeas

———————

2 tablespoons and
1 tablespoon olive oil, divided

1 white onion, halved and
thinly sliced

4 garlic cloves, very thinly
sliced or minced

¼ cup / 50g chopped
preserved lemon

1 teaspoon minced
fresh ginger

1 teaspoon ground turmeric

½ teaspoon sweet paprika

½ teaspoon ground cumin

4 carrots, trimmed, halved
lengthwise, and cut crosswise
into 2-inch / 5cm pieces

1 large or 2 small zucchini,
trimmed, quartered
lengthwise, and cut crosswise
into 2-inch / 5cm pieces

3 yellow potatoes (about
2½ inches / 6.5cm in
diameter), scrubbed and
quartered

1½ cups / 240g
cooked chickpeas, or
1 (15-ounce/425g) can
chickpeas, drained and rinsed

⅓ cup / 55g pitted and
halved Kalamata olives

⅓ cup / 55g pitted and
halved green olives

1⅔ cups / 395ml and 1⅓ cups
/ 395ml vegetable broth,
divided

1⅓ cups / 175g frozen green
peas, thawed

Salt and freshly ground
black pepper

1 cup / 180g couscous

COUSCOUS, CHICKPEAS, AND ZUCCHINI WITH PRESERVED LEMON AND OLIVES

A couple summers ago, I found myself at a Moroccan restaurant in the South of France. In spite of the blazing hot weather, I ordered and ate the best tagine I've ever tasted. It was a mix of carrots, green peas, and zucchini, with salty green olives and—the real treasure—pieces of preserved lemon, which I later learned were made in house. I piled the piping-hot ingredients over fluffy couscous and topped them with the salty Marcona almonds that came with my dinner. I think fondly of that meal—and daydream about sundrenched Provence—when I simmer this lemony one-pot stew at home. I like adding parsley and almonds as a finishing touch.

In a heavy-bottomed large pot, heat 2 tablespoons olive oil over medium heat. Add the onion and sauté, stirring frequently, for 4 to 5 minutes, until the onion is softening and translucent. Stir in the garlic. Cook for 1 more minute, stirring constantly, until the garlic is fragrant. Add the preserved lemon, ginger, turmeric, paprika, and cumin and stir to combine.

Add the carrots, zucchini, potatoes, chickpeas, both types of olives, and 1⅔ cups / 395ml of the broth to the pot. Raise the heat to high and bring the mixture to a simmer. Turn the heat to low, cover, and simmer for 20 minutes, stirring occasionally, until the carrots and potatoes are both tender when pierced with a fork. Stir in the peas, re-cover, and simmer for another 5 minutes. Taste the stew and add salt and pepper to your liking.

While the stew cooks, bring the remaining 1⅓ cups / 315ml broth, the remaining 1 tablespoon olive oil, and ¼ teaspoon of salt to a boil in a medium saucepan. Add the couscous, stir, and remove from the heat. Cover the pot and allow the couscous to steam for 5 minutes. Fluff the couscous with a fork.

To serve, divide the couscous among four bowls. Add one-fourth of the stew to each bowl, then top each with 1 tablespoon of the parsley and almonds (if using). The stew and couscous can be stored in airtight containers in the fridge for up to 5 days and frozen for up to 1 week.

Makes 4 to 6 servings of stew and 12 muffins

Grain: cornbread muffins
Green: collard greens
Bean: black-eyed peas

———————

CORNBREAD MUFFINS

1 tablespoon freshly squeezed lemon juice or apple cider vinegar

1¾ cups / 415ml unsweetened soy, oat, almond, or cashew milk

1¾ cups / 210g unbleached all-purpose flour

1¼ cups / 175g yellow cornmeal

3 tablespoons sugar

1 teaspoon baking powder

¾ teaspoon baking soda

½ teaspoon salt

8 tablespoons / 120ml melted vegan butter or avocado oil

STEW

1 tablespoon avocado oil

1 large white or yellow onion, chopped

2 garlic cloves, minced

1½ teaspoons smoked paprika

½ teaspoon ground cumin

1 (28-ounce / 800g) can diced tomatoes, preferably fire-roasted, with their juices

4 cups / 950ml vegetable broth

1 cup / 240ml water

¼ teaspoon salt, or more as needed

3 cups / 480g cooked black-eyed peas, drained

2 large sweet potatoes, peeled and diced (about 1 pound / 455g)

CORNBREAD MUFFINS, SMOKY BLACK-EYED PEAS, AND COLLARD GREENS

Black-eyed peas, collard greens, and rice are the main ingredients in hoppin' John, a dish that's eaten for good luck on New Year's Day in the U.S. Southeast. I make my own black-eyed pea dish for the new year in the form of this nourishing, smoky stew. I substitute sweet potatoes for the traditional rice, and I serve the soup with another of my favorite Southern foods: cornbread. While I like a batch of traditional cornbread, I love the puffy, cracked golden tops of these cornbread muffins and how conveniently portioned and easy to meal-prep they are.

Preheat the oven to 350°F/175°C. Line a regular muffin pan with liners or use a nonstick muffin pan.

Prepare the muffins. In a small bowl, combine the lemon juice and non-dairy milk. In a large bowl, whisk together the flour, cornmeal, sugar, baking powder, baking soda, and salt. Make a well in the center of the dry ingredients, then pour in the lemon juice mixture and the melted butter. Use a spatula or spoon to mix the ingredients into a batter. The batter should be mostly smooth, with no streaks of flour visible, but a few small lumps are okay.

Fill the prepared muffin cups three-quarters of the way to the top with the batter. Bake the muffins for 18 to 22 minutes, until they're domed and turning golden on top; a toothpick inserted in the center of a muffin should emerge clean. Transfer the muffins to a cooling rack.

Prepare the stew. Heat the avocado oil in a heavy-bottomed large pot over medium heat. When the oil is shimmering, add the onion. Sauté the onion, stirring occasionally, for 4 to 5 minutes, until translucent and tender. Add the garlic, paprika, and cumin. Continue to cook for 1 minute, until the garlic and spices are fragrant, stirring constantly.

Add the tomatoes, broth, water, salt, black-eyed peas, and sweet potatoes to the pot. Bring the mixture to a boil. Turn the heat to low, cover, and simmer for 10 minutes, until the sweet potatoes are tender. Add the collard greens to the pot, re-cover, and simmer for another 8 to 10 minutes, until the collard greens are tender. Taste the soup and add additional salt and the red pepper flakes to taste.

Transfer the soup to bowls, serving each portion with a cornmeal muffin. The stew can be stored in an airtight container in the fridge for up to 6 days. It can also be frozen for up to 6 weeks. The cornmeal muffins will keep in an airtight container at room temperature for up to 2 days; if you need to store them longer, wrap for freezing and freeze for up to 6 weeks.

1 small to medium bunch collard greens, thick bottom stems trimmed, remainder roughly chopped

Red pepper flakes

Makes 6 servings

Grain: white basmati rice
Green: dark leafy greens
Bean: yellow split peas

———————

6 cups / 1.4L water

1 cup / 200g yellow split peas, soaked overnight

1 cup / 140g diced carrots

¾ teaspoon ground turmeric

½ teaspoon ground coriander

½ teaspoon ground cumin

2 teaspoons finely minced fresh ginger

1 cup / 180g white basmati rice, rinsed (or white jasmine rice)

1¼ teaspoons salt

2 tablespoons avocado oil

2 teaspoons cumin seeds

2 teaspoons mustard seeds

4 cups / 80g stemmed and chopped dark leafy greens (such as kale, chard, mustard greens, beet greens, spinach)

1 cup / 240ml Cashew Sour Cream (page 216; optional), for serving

YELLOW SPLIT PEA AND BASMATI RICE PORRIDGE

This may be the most minimalist preparation of grains, greens, and beans in this book. The dish is inspired by kitchari, a porridge-like mixture of grains and legumes that's popular in India and is an important recipe in the Ayurvedic tradition. Kitchari can be made with a few types of beans, split peas, or lentils, and the grain is typically basmati rice, as it is here. I took all sorts of liberties with kitchari when I first learned about it, adding sautéed members of the onion family—which is not traditional—and using freewheeling mixtures of spices. Over time, I've come to rely on a pared-down, more traditional approach; I prefer its simplicity. My favorite legume to use here is toor dal, which most Americans know as yellow split peas. The peas retain enough firmness to give the porridge some texture, as well as offering a beautiful golden color. As with green split peas, soak these legumes overnight in water in the fridge. This will ensure they cook consistently and in a reasonable time. If you can't find yellow split peas, red or yellow lentils are a good substitute; just reduce the initial simmering time to 15 minutes before you add the rice.

In a heavy-bottomed large pot, bring the water to a boil over high heat. Add the soaked split peas, carrots, turmeric, coriander, cumin, and ginger. When the water returns to a boil, turn the heat to low, cover, and simmer for 30 minutes.

Add the rice and salt to the pot. Re-cover and continue simmering for 20 to 30 minutes, until the rice and split peas are both tender and the mixture resembles a porridge—thick and soupy. (You can adjust the consistency to your liking by adding water at this point, from 7 to 8 cups / 1.6 to 1.9L, if opting for a looser mixture.)

In a small frying pan, heat the avocado oil over medium-low heat. Add the cumin and mustard seeds and warm them, stirring occasionally, for 4 to 5 minutes, until fragrant and just starting to pop, but not browning or burning. Stir this mixture into the porridge along with the greens. Cover the pot and simmer for 5 more minutes.

Divide the porridge among six bowls. Enjoy plain or stir in some Cashew Sour Cream (if using). The porridge will keep in an airtight container in the fridge for up to 6 days and can be frozen for up to 6 weeks.

CREAMY CAVATAPPI, SMOKY TVP, AND YOUR FAVORITE FROZEN GREEN VEGETABLE

Makes 4 servings

Grain: cavatappi
Green: broccoli
Bean: TVP

———————

This is an easygoing meal you can make with pantry ingredients—pasta, tomato paste, cashews, and TVP—and a bag of some frozen green vegetable. In other words, it's the kind of recipe we all need more of. It's proudly inspired by Hamburger Helper, but TVP replaces the hamburger and Cashew Sour Cream enriches the sauce. I add a pop of green with a frozen vegetable; frozen broccoli florets, green peas, or chopped green beans are ones I always have in my freezer. Of course, if you have fresh baby spinach or zucchini or broccoli you'd like to use instead, try that option. And if you don't have the beef-style broth on hand, substitute chicken style or vegetable broth.

Bring 1½ cups / 360ml of the broth to a boil in a small pot (or microwave in a heatproof liquid measuring cup for 3 minutes, until bubbling). Place the TVP in a small bowl and pour the hot broth over it. Allow the broth to rehydrate the TVP for 10 minutes, then tilt the bowl to pour out extra broth. (No need to press the TVP or wring out all the moisture.)

In a large, deep skillet, heat the olive oil over medium heat. Add the onion and sauté for 5 to 6 minutes, stirring frequently, until translucent and starting to lightly brown. Stir in the tomato paste, chili powder, paprika, garlic powder, and salt. Add the TVP and stir everything well. Allow the protein to sizzle for 2 minutes without stirring, so it starts to firm up. Continue to cook, stirring occasionally, for 4 to 6 minutes, until the TVP is firmly chewy and browning a little.

Add the remaining 5 cups / 1.2L broth and the cavatappi. Bring the mixture to a boil, then cover the skillet. Turn the heat to low and simmer the dish for 20 minutes, until the pasta is just tender. Stir in the Cashew Sour Cream and nutritional yeast, then add the green vegetable. Re-cover the skillet and simmer for 5 more minutes, until the vegetable is hot and cooked through.

Stir and taste the pasta, and add additional salt and freshly ground black pepper to taste. Serve. The sauced pasta can be stored in an airtight container in the fridge for up to 5 days.

1½ cups / 360ml and 5 cups / 1.2L vegan beef-style broth, divided

1 cup / 100g TVP

1 tablespoon olive oil

1 small or ½ large white or yellow onion, finely diced

3 tablespoons / 45g tomato paste

½ teaspoon chili powder

¾ teaspoon smoked paprika

½ teaspoon garlic powder

¼ teaspoon salt, or more as needed

8 ounces / 225g cavatappi (or macaroni, shells, or fusilli)

⅓ cup / 80ml Cashew Sour Cream (page 216)

2 tablespoons nutritional yeast

1½ cups / 130g frozen broccoli florets or cuts, green peas, or cut green beans, thawed

Freshly ground black pepper

Makes 4 servings

Grain: white corn tortillas
Green: spinach
Bean: pinto beans

_____

8 (6-inch / 15cm) white corn tortillas

1 tablespoon and 1 tablespoon avocado oil, divided (or 1 tablespoon avocado oil and avocado oil spray)

1 small white or yellow onion, chopped

1½ cups / 240g cooked pinto beans, or 1 (15-ounce / 425g) can pinto beans, drained and rinsed

4 cups / 80g lightly packed fresh spinach leaves

1 (15-ounce / 425g) can red or green enchilada sauce

½ cup / 120ml restaurant-style salsa, mild or spicy

OPTIONAL TOPPING

1 cup / 185g crumbed Cheesy Tofu (page 210)

Cashew Sour Cream (page 216)

Guacamole (page 221) or shredded vegan cheese

1 cup / 40g chopped fresh cilantro

1 cup / 130g cooked corn kernels

½ cup / 65g store-bought pickled jalapeños or Quick Pickled Onions (page 208)

SAUCY STOVETOP TORTILLAS
WITH PINTO BEANS AND SPINACH

These skillet tortillas use store-bought enchilada sauce for simmering, which makes them an especially convenient option for last-minute savory breakfasts or brunches. You can transform the meal repeatedly by experimenting with different toppings, be they creamy, melty, crispy, or crumbly. I give a few of my favorite options in the ingredient list, but don't be afraid to add your own finishing touches! Note that the recipe calls for white corn tortillas, rather than yellow; white tortillas tend to be thinner and more pliable, which makes them especially good for soaking up the sauce.

Preheat the oven to 375°F / 190°C. Line a sheet pan with parchment paper or use a nonstick sheet pan.

On a cutting board, stack the tortillas and cut them into quarters. Arrange the tortillas on the prepared sheet pan. Brush them lightly on both sides with 1 tablespoon of the avocado oil to coat them lightly (or use cooking spray). Place in the oven and bake the chips for 10 to 12 minutes, until they're browning and crispy.

In a large, deep skillet, heat the remaining tablespoon avocado oil over medium heat. Add the onion and sauté, stirring often, for 5 to 6 minutes, until soft and translucent. Add the beans and spinach. Continue sautéing, stirring often, for 4 to 5 minutes, until the spinach is wilted and tender.

Turn the heat to medium low. Add the enchilada sauce and salsa to the skillet, followed by the tortilla quarters. Gently fold everything together—you may need a pair of tongs to help you—coating the tortilla chips with the sauce and mixing them with the beans and greens. Simmer the mixture for 3 to 5 minutes, until the chips have absorbed most of the sauce and are softening.

Top the skillet with your chosen toppings. Divide the mixture among four plates and enjoy. The saucy tortillas will keep in an airtight container in the fridge for up to 4 days.

CREAMY GOCHUJANG PASTA WITH GREEN ONIONS, KALE, AND EDAMAME

Makes 4 servings

Grain: bucatini pasta
Green: green onions, kale
Bean: edamame

---

8 ounces / 225g bucatini, long fusilli, malfadini, or other long pasta

2 garlic cloves, minced

3 tablespoons gochujang

¼ cup / 60g tahini

1 tablespoon unseasoned rice vinegar

2 tablespoons soy sauce

1 tablespoon avocado oil

4 green onions, white and green parts, chopped

2 cups / 50g sliced Tuscan kale (in thin ribbons)

1 cup / 150g frozen edamame, heated according to package instructions

Toasted sesame seeds, crumbled toasted nori, or vegan furikake seasoning, for topping (optional)

This is another combination of noodles and a gochujang-seasoned sauce. Whereas the kimchi noodle bowls on page 65 are served cold, this one-pot pasta is served hot, with a sauce that relies on tahini for its creamy texture—a genius touch that was inspired by Zaynab Issa's Gochujang-Sesame Noodles for *Bon Appetit*. The sauce is the star of the show, but a few toppings make this dish complete: the edamame and a sprinkle of crumbled seaweed, toasted sesame seeds, or store-bought furikake seasoning, which contains both. Furikake isn't always vegan, but a few brands, including Watson's, Nori Komi, and Jacobson Salt Co., make vegan versions.

Bring a large pot of salted water to a boil. Cook the pasta according to package instructions, until it's a desired consistency. Reserve 1 cup / 240ml of the cooking water and drain the pasta in a colander. Set aside.

In a small bowl, whisk together the garlic, gochujang, tahini, rice vinegar, and soy sauce. Return the large pot to the stove, add the avocado oil, and warm it over medium heat. Add the green onions and kale and sauté for 2 to 3 minutes, until the green onions are tender and the kale is tender yet still a vibrant green. Add the gochujang mixture to the pot, along with about half the reserved cooking water, and stir well. Add the pasta to the pot and stir to coat the pasta with the creamy sauce. Continue adding additional small amounts of pasta water until desired consistency. The pasta should be creamy but not soupy.

Divide the pasta among four bowls. Top each bowl with one-fourth of the edamame and a generous amount of the sesame seeds, crumbled nori, or furikake (if using). Enjoy at once. The pasta and sauce can be stored in an airtight container in the fridge for up to 3 days.

Before I assembled this recipe collection, I had no idea how easy it can be to cook grains in the oven. There's no need to babysit a pot or sauté pan, and oven-cooking reduces the likelihood of burnt bottom layers. In some cases, baked grains are fluffier than grains simmered in a pot; the coconut rice on page 172 is a perfect example.

Oven-baked grains make frequent appearances in this section, which comprises mostly sheet-pan meals and casseroles. To prepare these dishes, you'll need a few hardworking pieces of cookware: an 8-inch / 20cm square baking pan, a 9 by 13-inch / 23 by 33cm rectangular baking pan, and two half-size (18 by 13-inch / 45 by 33cm) sheet pans. If you don't have two sheet pans, then you can stagger the cooking process, cooling and cleaning the pans between uses.

Grains bake more efficiently when you add hot liquid, rather than cold, before you place them in the oven. You can bring water or broth to a simmer in a saucepan and add it to the sheet pan or casserole dish. Or, you can use a shortcut—my personal preference—and fill a large heatproof liquid measuring cup with the water or broth, cover it with a microwave-safe plate, and microwave it on high for 4 to 6 minutes. This is usually enough time to bring the liquid to a gentle simmer, at which point you can add it to the grains.

Some oven-baked grains need to be covered while they cook. I like to use foil for this, and I'm always careful to tightly wrap the foil around the edges of the baking pan. If you have an oven-safe silicone cover to use instead, that's fine.

My favorite thing about baking or roasting is the little break that comes after I've popped something into the oven and set the timer. Baking and roasting require work, of course, but they offer opportunities to turn away from the kitchen and think about something other than what's cooking. Maybe you'll use that time to clean up a little, maybe you'll tend to a child with a homework question, maybe you'll text a friend. No matter what you do, you'll have a chance—maybe a few chances—to pause, all while knowing that a nutritious meal is on its way to your table.

OVEN TO TABLE RECIPES

Makes 4 servings

Grain: rye bread

Green: green cabbage, Swiss chard

Bean: butter beans

2 large or 3 slices rye bread or sourdough bread

1 tablespoon and 1½ tablespoons avocado oil, divided

Fine sea salt

1 small head green cabbage

¼ teaspoon garlic powder

Freshly ground black pepper

2 tablespoons olive oil

4 garlic cloves, very thinly sliced

1½ cups cooked butter beans, or 1 (15-ounce / 425g) can butter beans

1 teaspoon grated lemon zest

1½ tablespoons freshly squeezed lemon juice, or more as needed

1 scant tablespoon minced fresh rosemary

4 cups / 80g finely chopped green Swiss chard, curly kale, Tuscan kale, or spinach, or 4 cups / 80g fresh baby spinach

¼ cup / 60ml vegetable broth

Red pepper flakes

4 tablespoons / 30g Cheesy Topping (page 209), or a drizzle of Tahini Sauce (page 214) (optional)

CABBAGE STEAKS WITH ROSEMARY BUTTER BEANS AND BREAD CRUMBS

I so love the idea of cabbage steaks, cauliflower steaks, and other vegetable "steaks," all of which are hearty slabs of vegetables that are roasted or sautéed and served as vegan entrées. What's un-steaklike about these juicy cuts of vegetables, however, is their limited amount of protein. Of course, that's nothing the addition of a bean won't fix. In this recipe, tender roasted cabbage steaks are topped with butter beans that have been sautéed with lemon, rosemary, and a dark leafy green of your choosing. The grain here is a crispy heap of rustic whole-grain bread crumbs. While it's common to add butter or oil to make bread crumbs, I prefer to dry-roast them, which then allows them to soak up more flavor when they're added to dishes.

Preheat the oven to 400°F / 200°C.

Place the bread slices in a food processor and pulse until roughly ground, a little bigger than commercial bread crumbs. Spread the crumbs on a sheet pan, then drizzle them with the tablespoon of avocado oil and a pinch of salt. Mix well to coat them with the oil.

Line another sheet pan with aluminum foil or parchment paper or use a nonstick sheet pan.

Trim the top of the cabbage head and its thick bottom stem. Cut the cabbage crosswise into 1-inch / 2.5cm slices. These may fall apart a bit as you work, but that's okay. Just try to get four even, intact slices to serve as steaks. Place the steaks on the prepared sheet pan, arranging smaller leftover pieces of the cabbage head around them, and drizzle the cabbage with the remaining 1½ tablespoons avocado oil. Use your hands (or a pastry brush) to rub the steaks with the oil, coating them evenly on their top and bottom sides. Sprinkle the tops with the garlic powder, ½ teaspoon of salt, and black pepper to your liking. Place the steaks in the oven and roast for 25 to 30 minutes, until they are completely tender and the outer leaves are browning and crispy. It's not necessary to flip the steaks during roasting—and they may fall apart if you try—but do rotate the sheet pan once halfway through roasting.

CONTINUED

CABBAGE STEAKS WITH ROSEMARY BUTTER BEANS
AND BREAD CRUMBS, CONTINUED

In the last 10 minutes of roasting, add the sheet pan with the bread crumbs to the oven. Roast the bread crumbs for 8 to 10 minutes, until a deep golden brown.

Meanwhile, heat the olive oil in a large, deep skillet over medium-low heat. Add the garlic and sauté for 2 minutes, stirring the whole time, until fragrant. Add the butter beans, lemon zest and juice, rosemary, and ¼ teaspoon salt. Continue to sauté the beans for 2 minutes, until they're warmed through and softened. Add the greens to the skillet along with the broth. Turn the heat to low and simmer the greens, stirring often, for 3 to 10 minutes, until tender yet still a vibrant green. (Baby spinach will likely need only a few minutes, while kale or chard may need longer.) Taste the bean-and-green mixture and add additional lemon juice and salt, as well as the red pepper to taste.

To serve, divide the cabbage steaks among four plates. Top each with one-fourth of the bean-and-green mixture, followed by one-fourth of the crispy bread crumbs. If desired, add a tablespoon of the Cheesy Topping or drizzle the steaks with the Tahini Sauce (depending on whether you'd like additional texture or want a saucier dish). Serve. The cabbage steaks and the bean-and-green mixture will keep in separate airtight containers in the fridge for up to 4 days. Combine them when you're ready to eat. The bread crumbs can be stored in an airtight container at room temperature for up to 1 week.

STUFFED BELL PEPPERS WITH RICE, SEASONED SOY PROTEIN, AND CHARD

Makes 4 servings

Grain: long-grain white rice
Green: Swiss chard
Bean: TVP

I love a stuffed pepper! Regardless of what you decide to put into it, there's something about using the pepper as a cooking vessel that makes a meal feel special. Plus, red, orange, and yellow bell peppers yield sweet, flavorful juices as they bake, which mingle with whatever ingredients they've been stuffed with. For this recipe, that stuffing is a mixture of rice and TVP flavored with onion and taco seasoning. Most stuffed-pepper recipes call for a layer of melted cheese on top, and you could opt for vegan cheese shreds as a topping here if you're a stickler for tradition. I prefer a spoonful of homemade guacamole, which adds flavor and creaminess, as well as a pop of color. Note that the tops of the peppers are sliced off so as to open the peppers for stuffing. Rather than wasting those tops, I chop and add them to the filling.

8 red, orange, or yellow bell peppers

1 tablespoon avocado oil

1 small white or yellow onion, chopped

1 cup / 100g TVP

4 tablespoons / 30g taco seasoning, spicy or mild

1½ cups / 360ml vegetable broth

1 cup / 180g long-grain white rice

1 (14½-ounce / 415g) can diced fire-roasted tomatoes, with their juices

1½ cups / 360ml water

1 small bunch green or rainbow Swiss chard, ribs removed and leaves chopped

1 to 2 tablespoons freshly squeezed lime juice

Salt

3 cups / 560g Guacamole (page 221) (or chopped or sliced Hass avocado, or plant-based cheddar or pepper jack cheese)

Preheat the oven to 375°F / 190°C. Lightly oil the bottom of a 9 by 13-inch / 23 by 33cm baking pan with 2½-inch / 6cm sides.

Slice the very tops off the bell peppers, including the stems. Finely chop the tops and set aside. Remove the core and seeds from inside the peppers. Place the hollowed-out peppers, cut side up, in the baking pan. Place the peppers in the oven and bake for 30 minutes, until tender but not yet collapsing. Set aside and let cool slightly.

Meanwhile, heat the avocado oil in a large, deep skillet over medium heat. Add the onion and the reserved chopped peppers. Cook, stirring occasionally, for 5 to 7 minutes, until the onion is tender and translucent. Add the TVP, taco seasoning, and broth to the skillet and stir. Bring the broth to a simmer, then simmer, uncovered, for 6 to 7 minutes, until the TVP has absorbed the broth and is starting to brown.

Add the rice, tomatoes, and water to the skillet and turn the heat to high. When the liquid begins to simmer, cover the skillet and turn the heat to low. Cook for 10 minutes, then uncover the skillet and add the chard. Re-cover the skillet and continue cooking for 10 more minutes, until the greens and rice are both tender and the liquid has been entirely absorbed. Add the lime juice to taste. Stir the mixture, taste it, and season as needed with salt.

CONTINUED

STUFFED BELL PEPPERS WITH RICE, SEASONED
SOY PROTEIN, AND CHARD, CONTINUED

Fill the cooked peppers with the rice and TVP mixture. Return the peppers to the oven and bake for an additional 10 minutes. (This step warms the peppers again and gives the rice a chance to absorb some of the pepper juices.)

Remove the peppers from the oven and top each with a spoonful of Guacamole. Serve. The peppers can be par-baked and the filling can be prepared up to 3 days before stuffing. Baked stuffed peppers will keep in an airtight container in the fridge for up to 5 days and can be frozen for up to 6 weeks.

Makes 6 servings

Grain: sushi rice
Green: green onions, cucumber, spinach
Bean: tofu

---

2 cups / 480ml water

1 cup / 180g sushi rice or short-grain white rice, soaked for at least 1 hour, then drained and rinsed

1½ tablespoons and 2 tablespoons unseasoned rice vinegar, divided

2 teaspoons cane sugar

½ teaspoon fine sea salt

1 teaspoon toasted sesame oil

1 bunch green onions, green and white parts, thinly sliced crosswise

4 cups / 80g lightly packed fresh baby spinach

¾ cup / 170g vegan mayonnaise or Cashew Sour Cream (page 216)

2 tablespoons sriracha or other hot sauce

1 tablespoon soy sauce

1 (14-ounce / 400g) block super-firm or extra-firm tofu, pressed (see page 212) and cut into ½-inch / 1.3cm cubes

Avocado oil, for baking pan

½ cup / 45g vegan furikake

1 cup / 100g thinly sliced cucumber

1 small avocado, halved, pitted, and thinly sliced lengthwise into slivers

Roasted salted nori sheets, for serving (optional)

BAKED SUSHI RICE, TOFU, AND SPINACH WITH NORI AND FURIKAKE SEASONING

The viral sushi bake is a deconstructed version of the classic California sushi roll that's served hot. Imitation crab salad, sushi rice, and furikake or toasted nori sheets are layered and baked until warm. This plant-based version replaces the imitation crab with a creamy tofu mayonnaise salad, and it adds a green component with a layer of lightly sautéed spinach and green onions. The most fun part of making this bake is decorating it with thin avocado slices, sliced cucumber, and a generous zigzag drizzle of sriracha mayo. You can simply slice the sushi bake into squares and enjoy as is, or you can scoop your portion onto sheets of toasted nori for extra crunch.

Preheat the oven to 350°F / 175°C.

In a medium saucepan, bring the water and rice to a simmer over medium-high heat. Cover the saucepan and turn the heat to low. Simmer the rice for 15 minutes, until the water is absorbed and the rice is tender. Remove the saucepan from the heat and set aside, still covered, for 10 minutes.

Whisk together the 1½ tablespoons vinegar, the sugar, and salt in a small bowl. Pour this mixture over the rice, then use a rice paddle or a wooden spoon to gently fluff the rice and incorporate the seasonings. Cover the rice again and set aside.

In a deep medium skillet, heat the sesame oil over medium heat. When the oil is hot, add the green onions and sauté, stirring frequently, for 3 minutes, until the white parts are translucent and tender. Add the spinach in handfuls and continue cooking for another 2 to 3 minutes, stirring often, until the spinach is fully wilted and tender.

In a large bowl, whisk together the mayonnaise, sriracha, the remaining 2 tablespoons rice vinegar, and the soy sauce. Transfer ⅓ cup / 80ml of this mixture to a small bowl and set aside. Then, add the cubed tofu to the bowl and gently mix with the remaining sauce until evenly incorporated.

Lightly oil the bottom of an 8-inch / 20cm square baking pan. Using a spoon or spatula, spread the rice in the bottom of the baking pan in an even layer. Distribute the spinach and green onions over the rice, then

sprinkle half the furikake over the greens. Next, spread the tofu mixture over the greens layer, followed by the remaining furikake. Place the baking pan in the oven and bake for 15 to 20 minutes, until the top is hot and bubbling.

Allow the sushi bake to cool for 10 minutes, then top it with the cucumber and avocado slices and drizzle with the remaining sriracha mayonnaise. Cut the bake into squares and serve. If desired, scoop out the bake and place on top of roasted salty pieces of nori. The sushi bake can be stored in the fridge for up to 4 days.

Makes 6 servings

Grain: lasagna noodles
Green: spinach
Bean: tofu

──────────

VEGAN RICOTTA

¾ cup / 105g unroasted cashews, soaked for at least 2 hours and drained

2 tablespoons water

1 tablespoon freshly squeezed lemon juice, or more as needed

2 tablespoons nutritional yeast

1 teaspoon salt, or more as needed

¼ teaspoon garlic powder

Pinch freshly ground black pepper, or more as needed

14 ounces / 400g extra-firm tofu, pressed gently between tea towels or paper towels to remove moisture

16 lasagna noodles (12 needed, with extra for breaking or tearing)

10 ounces / 300g frozen chopped spinach, cooked according to package instructions and drained

2½ cups / 590ml store-bought marinara sauce

LASAGNA ROLLS WITH TOFU CASHEW RICOTTA AND SPINACH

I have a deep, abiding love for classic lasagna (made vegan, of course). For a meal prepper like me, lasagna rolls make even more sense than the traditional, layered pasta dish. They're easy to portion, which also makes them easy to serve, store, and freeze for your future self. Altogether, this is both a nutrient- and a protein-rich recipe, but it's pure comfort to eat.

Prepare the vegan ricotta. Place the cashews in a food processor fitted with the S blade. Add the water, lemon juice, nutritional yeast, salt, garlic powder, and pepper. Pulse a few times, then process for about 1 minute, until coarsely ground.

Crumble the tofu into the food processor. Process for another 2 minutes, stopping a few times to scrape down the sides of the bowl, until the tofu is creamy and smooth. Taste and adjust the salt, pepper, and lemon to your liking.

Preheat the oven to 350°F / 175°C. Lightly oil a 9 by 13-inch / 23 by 33cm baking pan with 2½-inch / 6cm sides.

Bring a large pot of salted water to boil. Add the lasagna sheets and cook according to package instructions (usually 10 to 12 minutes), until tender.

Place the ricotta in a large bowl and add the spinach. Mix well.

Pour about ¾ cup / 180ml of the marinara sauce into the prepared baking pan, then spread it evenly on the bottom of the pan.

Line a work surface with parchment paper, wax paper, or aluminum foil. Place 1 lasagna noodle in the middle. Top with ¼ cup / 60ml of the vegan ricotta and spread it evenly along the noodle. Add 1 tablespoon of the marinara sauce and spread the sauce lightly over the ricotta. Starting at the short end of the noodle, roll the lasagna noodle up. Place the roll seam side down in the baking pan. Repeat with the remaining noodles, ricotta, and sauce, arranging the rolls in rows in the baking pan. Spoon the remaining sauce over the rolls.

Cover the baking pan with foil and place in the oven. Bake for 15 minutes, then remove the foil and bake for another 15 to 20 minutes, until the sauce has darkened and is bubbling at the edges. Serve. The cooked lasagna rolls can be kept in an airtight container in the fridge for up to 5 days and frozen for up to 8 weeks.

Makes 4 servings

Grain: white basmati rice
Green: baby spinach,
green peas
Bean: chickpeas

_____

COCONUT RICE

1 cup / 180g white
basmati rice

¾ cup / 180ml full-fat canned
coconut milk

1½ cups / 360ml water

¼ teaspoon salt

CAULIFLOWER AND
CHICKPEAS

1 small cauliflower, stem
trimmed, broken into bite-
sized florets and pieces
(about 12 ounces / 340g)

1½ cups / 240g
cooked chickpeas, or
1 (15-ounce/425g) can
chickpeas, drained and rinsed

2 tablespoons avocado oil

1 teaspoon ground turmeric

1 teaspoon ground cumin

½ teaspoon ground ginger

½ teaspoon garlic powder

½ teaspoon salt

⅛ teaspoon freshly ground
black pepper

½ cup / 85g frozen green
peas, thawed

3 cups / 60g lightly packed
fresh baby spinach leaves

SAUCE

1 cup / 240ml Cashew Sour
Cream (page 216) or store-
bought vegan yogurt

½ teaspoon salt

½ teaspoon ground cumin

1 garlic clove, finely minced
or grated

COCONUT RICE WITH ROASTED CAULIFLOWER, CHICKPEAS, AND SPINACH

I can make this baked coconut rice over and over. It's irresistibly fluffy and has a lovely, subtle coconut fragrance when it comes out of the oven. The rice is a perfect pillow for a generous portion of crispy baked chickpeas and cauliflower, which are seasoned (and stained a bright gold) with turmeric, cumin, and ginger. The sauce, which adds texture, temperature, and flavor contrast, is inspired by raita, a cooling dish of yogurt and vegetables that can serve as a dip or a side dish. The raita uses my Cashew Sour Cream as its base, but if you like, substitute store-bought vegan yogurt.

Preheat the oven to 400°F / 200°C.

Prepare the rice. Place the rice in a medium bowl and fill it with water. Swish the rice around with your fingers a little to help release some of the rice's natural starch, then rinse in a fine-mesh strainer under cold running water for about a minute. Allow it to drain and repeat once more.

Place the rice, coconut milk, water, and salt in an 8-inch / 20cm square baking pan. Cover the pan tightly with foil.

Prepare the cauliflower and chickpeas. Place the cauliflower and chickpeas in a 9 by 13-inch / 23 by 33cm baking pan with 2½-inch / 6cm sides. Drizzle the mixture with the avocado oil, then sprinkle the turmeric, cumin, ginger, garlic powder, salt, and pepper over it. Stir well, coating the vegetables with oil and distributing the spices.

Transfer both pans to the oven. Bake the rice for 30 minutes, or until it has absorbed the liquid and is tender and fluffy. Roast the cauliflower and chickpeas for 30 to 35 minutes, until the cauliflower is tender and crisping at the edges and the chickpeas become crispy. Stir the cauliflower and chickpeas once halfway through the roasting.

Arrange the peas and spinach on top of the baked rice, cover again, and bake for 5 minutes more. Uncover the baking pan and stir well to combine the ingredients.

While the rice and cauliflower are in the oven, prepare the sauce. In a small or medium bowl, combine the Cashew Sour Cream and the remaining sauce ingredients. Stir well to combine.

Divide the coconut rice and the cauliflower and chickpeas among four plates. Top each portion generously with some of the sauce. The baked rice, the cauliflower-chickpea mixture, and the sauce will keep separately in airtight containers in the fridge for up to 4 days.

2 tablespoons freshly squeezed lime juice

¾ cup / 105g peeled, seeded, and grated cucumber, squeezed through paper towels or cheesecloth to remove moisture

¼ cup / 10g finely chopped fresh mint

Makes 4 to 6 servings

Grain: rolled oats
Green: brussels sprouts
Bean: lentils

———————

LOAF

1 tablespoon olive oil

1 small white or yellow onion, diced

2 celery stalks, diced

2 carrots, peeled and diced

4 garlic cloves, finely minced

1 teaspoon dried thyme

½ teaspoon dried rosemary

½ teaspoon smoked paprika

1 teaspoon salt, or more as needed

¼ teaspoon freshly ground black pepper, or more as needed

2¾ cups / 650ml vegetable broth

1 cup / 90g dried green or brown lentils

1½ cups / 150g grated unpeeled sweet potato (about 1 potato)

1 cup / 100g old-fashioned rolled oats

¼ cup / 60g tomato paste

⅓ cup / 80g ketchup, plus extra for serving

ROASTED BRUSSELS SPROUTS

1½ pounds / 680g brussels sprouts, trimmed and halved lengthwise

2 tablespoons avocado oil

Salt

Red pepper flakes

1 tablespoon white or red balsamic vinegar (optional)

SWEET POTATO LENTIL LOAF AND ROASTED BRUSSELS SPROUTS

In 2011, I published a sweet potato–lentil loaf on my blog. I meant it to be a holiday recipe, but it quickly became a personal favorite, and I no longer wait for special occasions to make it. To turn this into a complete meal, you can roast some brussels sprouts while the lentil loaf rests. The meal requires some time, but it's worth the effort, especially if you are lucky enough to have leftover loaf slices to put into the sandwiches on page 114.

Prepare the loaf. Heat the olive oil in a heavy-bottomed large pot over medium heat. Add the onion, celery, and carrots and cook for 5 to 7 minutes, stirring often, until the onion is translucent. Add the garlic to the pot and cook, stirring constantly, for 1 more minute.

Add the thyme, rosemary, paprika, salt, pepper, broth, lentils, and sweet potato to the pot. Bring the mixture to a boil, then reduce the heat to low. Cover the pot and simmer until the lentils are tender, about 30 minutes.

Preheat the oven to 350°F / 175°C. Lightly oil an 8½ by 4½-inch / 21 by 10cm loaf pan with 2¾-inch / 6cm sides.

Stir the rolled oats and tomato paste into the pot, cover, and let rest for 5 minutes. The oats will absorb most of the remaining moisture and the mixture will thicken. Taste and adjust salt and pepper as needed.

Press the mixture into the loaf pan. Brush the top of the loaf with the ketchup. Cover the loaf pan with a tent of foil and bake for 20 minutes. Remove the foil and bake for another 20 minutes, until the loaf is firm and the ketchup has darkened. Set the loaf aside to cool at room temperature.

Increase the oven temperature to 400°F / 200°C.

Prepare the sprouts. Spread the brussels sprouts on one or two sheet pans in an even layer. Drizzle with the avocado oil and sprinkle with salt, then stir to coat the sprouts evenly with the oil. Place the sheet pans in the oven and roast for 35 minutes, until the sprouts are tender and turning golden and crispy on the outside. Stir the sprouts once halfway through roasting. Remove the sheet pans from the oven,

sprinkle the sprouts with the red pepper flakes, and drizzle with some vinegar (if using).

Cut the lentil loaf into slices, two or three slices per person. If you like, reheat these slices in the microwave or by transferring them to the still-hot oven in a covered dish for 5 minutes, or until sufficiently hot for your liking. Serve the slices with the roasted sprouts and some extra ketchup as desired. Leftover lentil loaf will keep in an airtight container in the fridge for up to 5 days. It can be frozen for up to 6 weeks. Leftover sprouts will keep in an airtight container in the fridge for up to 4 days.

Makes 4 servings

Grain: polenta
Green: broccoli rabe
Bean: cannellini beans

POLENTA

1 cup / 185g yellow corn coarse polenta

½ teaspoon salt

4 cups / 950 ml water

¾ cup / 180ml unsweetened soy, oat, almond, or cashew milk

2 to 3 tablespoons Cheesy Topping (page 209) or store-bought vegan parmesan cheese

1 pound / 450g fresh baby bella or cremini mushrooms, halved if large

1 tablespoon and 1 tablespoon olive oil, divided

3 tablespoons balsamic vinegar

1 tablespoon soy sauce

Freshly ground black pepper

2 garlic cloves, minced, and 4 garlic cloves, smashed, divided

1 bunch broccoli rabe, thick ends trimmed

½ teaspoon salt

Red pepper flakes

1½ cups / 280g cooked cannellini beans, or 1 (14.5-ounce / 415g) can cannellini beans, drained

Cheesy Topping (page 209; optional), for serving

Aged balsamic vinegar, for serving (optional)

BAKED POLENTA, WHITE BEANS, ROASTED MUSHROOMS, AND BROCCOLI RABE

If you're one of the many people who dislikes broccoli rabe, roasting it on a sheet pan might change your mind. The roasting brings out the green's natural sweetness and gives it some pleasantly crispy bits; it's also an easy preparation method. This recipe also features my favorite method of cooking polenta, which is to mix it with water and bake it, uncovered. It's every bit as simple as it sounds, and it produces a wonderfully creamy grain.

Preheat the oven to 350°F / 175°C.

Prepare the polenta. Place the polenta, salt, and water in an 8-inch / 20cm square baking pan. Place the pan in the oven and bake the polenta, uncovered, for 40 minutes. Stir in the non-dairy milk and a few tablespoons of the Cheesy Topping as desired, and bake, uncovered, for another 5 to 10 minutes, until the polenta is thick and creamy, yet easy to scoop and stir. Cover the polenta with foil and set aside.

Increase the oven heat to 425°F / 220°C. Line two sheet pans with parchment paper or aluminum foil or use nonstick sheet pans.

Place the mushrooms on one of the prepared sheet pans. In a small bowl, whisk together 1 tablespoon of the olive oil, the balsamic vinegar, soy sauce, a few turns of black pepper, and the minced garlic. Pour this over the mushrooms and mix well.

Place the broccoli rabe on the other prepared sheet pan, along with the smashed garlic cloves. Drizzle the greens with the remaining tablespoon olive oil and sprinkle with the salt and red pepper flakes. Use your hands to mix the greens with the oil.

Place both sheet pans in the oven. Roast the rabe for 10 to 12 minutes, until the leaves are browning and crispy and the stems are tender. Remove the rabe from the oven. Meanwhile, stir the mushrooms on the sheet pan; they'll have let out a lot of liquid at this point. Lower the oven heat to 400°F / 200°C and continue to roast the mushrooms for another 15 to 20 minutes, until tender and greatly reduced in size. Add the cannellini beans to the mushrooms.

In the last 5 minutes of roasting time, return the polenta to the oven to warm.

To serve, divide the polenta among four bowls. Top each portion with one-fourth of the rabe, the mushrooms, and the cannellini beans. Finish the bowls with the Cheesy Topping and a drizzle of balsamic vinegar (if using). Serve. The rabe, mushrooms, and polenta can be stored separately in airtight containers in the fridge for up to 4 days.

SHEET-PAN SHAWARMA-SPICED SOY CURLS AND FREEKEH

Makes 4 servings

Grain: freekeh
Green: zucchini, parsley
Bean: soy curls

———————

This is an incredibly flavorful dish of vegetables, a whole grain, and a "meaty" vegan protein, all cooked together on a single sheet pan, so the flavors have lots of opportunity to mingle. The added bonus? Cleanup is minimal! The only component missing is a sauce, and for that I like Tahini Sauce, which works well with the recipe's shawarma-inspired spice blend.

A quick note about the soy curls used in this recipe: They should be soaked and drained as directed, but skip the 10 minutes of baking included in the preparation on page 213.

Preheat the oven to 425°F / 220°C.

Arrange the soy curls, red onion, bell pepper, and zucchini on a sheet pan. In a small bowl or liquid measuring cup, whisk together the avocado oil, lemon juice, cumin, paprika, turmeric, coriander, cinnamon, allspice, and salt. Pour the mixture over the soy curls and vegetables, then use your hands to mix the ingredients well, so the soy curls and vegetables are well coated with the seasonings.

Place the sheet pan in the oven and roast for 22 to 25 minutes, until the soy curls are browning and becoming crispy and the vegetables are tender and browning.

Bring the broth to a boil in a saucepan over medium-high heat or by microwaving it on high in a heatproof liquid measuring cup for 5 minutes.

Add the freekeh to the sheet pan, then pour the hot broth over all. Stir the ingredients with a spoon or spatula, cover the pan tightly with foil, and return it to the oven for another 20 to 25 minutes, until the freekeh has absorbed the broth. Allow the sheet pan to rest, still covered with the foil, for 10 minutes.

Remove the foil from the sheet pan. Taste the ingredients and add the red pepper flakes (if desired), along with additional salt or lemon juice as needed. Divide the ingredients among four plates. Top each portion generously with some Tahini Sauce and garnish with the parsley, if using. Serve. The soy curls, freekeh, and vegetable mixture can be stored in an airtight container in the fridge for up to 5 days and frozen for up to 8 weeks.

1 batch (3 cups / 180g) Savory Soy Curls (page 213; see headnote)

1 large red onion, halved lengthwise and cut into ½-inch / 1.3cm slices

1 large red, orange, or yellow bell pepper, trimmed, cored, seeded, and sliced

2 small or 1 large zucchini, halved lengthwise, then cut into ⅜-inch / 1cm half-moons

2 tablespoons avocado oil

2 tablespoons freshly squeezed lemon juice, or more as needed

1 teaspoon ground cumin

½ teaspoon paprika

½ teaspoon ground turmeric

½ teaspoon ground coriander

¼ teaspoon ground cinnamon

⅛ teaspoon ground allspice

½ teaspoon salt, or more as needed

2¼ cups / 530ml vegetable broth

1 cup / 180g freekeh

Pinch red pepper flakes (optional)

¾ cup / 180ml Tahini Sauce (page 214)

Chopped fresh parsley, for garnish (optional)

½ medium or 1 small kabocha squash, halved, seeded, and cut into 1-inch / 2.5cm wedges

1½ tablespoons avocado oil

1 cup / 180g wild rice or a wild rice and brown rice blend

2 cups / 480ml water

¼ teaspoon salt

6 tablespoons / 90ml olive oil

1½ tablespoons white miso

3 tablespoons freshly squeezed lemon juice, or more as needed

1½ tablespoons soy sauce, or more as needed

1½ teaspoons toasted sesame oil

2 garlic cloves, finely minced or grated

1 small bunch Tuscan kale, stemmed and sliced crosswise into thin ribbons

¼ cup / 20g sliced green onions, green parts only

1½ cups / 240g cooked adzuki beans, or 1 (15-ounce / 425g) can adzuki beans, drained and rinsed

WILD RICE, ADZUKI BEANS, KABOCHA, AND KALE WITH MISO VINAIGRETTE

I'm partial to all members of the winter squash family, but my favorite by far is kabocha squash, or Japanese pumpkin. This type of squash has a denser, richer-tasting flesh than the others. This recipe spotlights roasted wedges of kabocha, which are arranged on a savory bed of oven-baked wild rice, adzuki beans, and kale.

Preheat the oven to 400°F / 220°C. Line a sheet pan with foil or use a nonstick sheet pan.

Arrange the squash on the sheet pan in a single layer. Drizzle the avocado oil over the squash and use your hands to mix well, so the wedges are all coated with oil.

Place the rice, water, and salt in an 8-inch / 20cm square baking pan. Cover the pan tightly with foil.

Place the sheet pan and baking pan in the oven. Roast the squash for 25 to 30 minutes, flipping the slices once halfway through the baking time. The slices should be tender and starting to turn golden brown in spots; you'll remove them from the oven before the rice finishes cooking. Cook the rice for 45 minutes in total, until it's tender and has absorbed all the water. Uncover the rice and fluff it gently with a fork.

While the squash and rice are cooking, whisk together the olive oil, miso, lemon juice, soy sauce, sesame oil, and garlic in a small bowl. Place the kale in a large bowl and add 3 tablespoons of this dressing. Use your hands to massage the dressing into the kale, so the kale becomes tender and glistens.

Add the cooked rice, green onion tops, and adzuki beans to the bowl with the kale, along with another 2 tablespoons of the dressing. Mix well, taste, and adjust the soy sauce and lemon juice as needed.

Divide the rice mixture among four plates or bowls. Top each portion of rice with one-fourth of the squash. Before serving, drizzle a little of the remaining dressing over the squash slices and rice. Enjoy. The squash slices and rice and kale mixture can be stored in separate airtight containers in the fridge for 4 and 3 days, respectively.

Makes 4 servings

Grain: millet
Green: collard greens
Bean: kidney beans

—————

1 cup / 180g millet

4 cups / 950ml vegetable broth

1 large white onion, halved lengthwise and cut into ¼-inch / 6mm slices

1 large green bell pepper, trimmed, cored, seeded, and cut into ¼-inch / 6mm slices

1 large red, orange, or yellow bell pepper, trimmed, cored, seeded, and cut into ¼-inch / 6mm slices

2 tablespoons avocado oil

1 teaspoon dried oregano

½ teaspoon smoked paprika

½ teaspoon and ¼ teaspoon salt, divided, plus more as desired

½ teaspoon onion powder

¼ teaspoon garlic powder

⅛ teaspoon and ⅛ teaspoon freshly ground black pepper, divided

Pinch cayenne

1 cup / 240ml unsweetened soy, oat, cashew, or almond milk

2 tablespoons nutritional yeast

1 (15-ounce / 425g) can dark red kidney beans, drained and rinsed

1 small bunch collard greens, stemmed, leaves cut into thin ribbons

1 tablespoon freshly squeezed lemon juice, or more as needed

BAKED MILLET WITH SHEET-PAN PEPPERS, ONIONS, KIDNEY BEANS, AND COLLARD GREENS

Oven-baking is my favorite way to prepare millet. The otherwise dry grain becomes creamy and tender, much like soft polenta, and it makes for a wonderful side dish. In this recipe, however, the millet is more of a centerpiece. I pile it high with spiced peppers and onions as well as kidney beans and collard greens. This is a dinner with lots of comfort-food appeal, brought to life with ultra-wholesome ingredients.

Preheat the oven to 400°F / 200°C. Line a sheet pan with aluminum foil or use a nonstick sheet pan.

Put a medium cast-iron or other ovenproof skillet over medium heat, then pour in the millet and toast it, stirring frequently, for 4 to 6 minutes, until the millet is browning lightly and some of the grains are popping. Pour the broth into the skillet. Cover the skillet tightly with foil.

Place the onion and pepper slices on the prepared sheet pan. Drizzle the avocado oil over the vegetables, then sprinkle with the oregano, paprika, ½ teaspoon of the salt, the onion and garlic powders, ⅛ teaspoon of the pepper, and the cayenne. Mix the vegetables well to coat with the seasonings.

Place both the skillet and the sheet pan in the oven. Bake the millet for 15 minutes, then uncover and stir. Bake for another 20 to 25 minutes, until the millet is firm at the edges and all the liquid has been absorbed. Stir in the non-dairy milk, remaining ¼ teaspoon salt and ⅛ teaspoon pepper, and the nutritional yeast. Re-cover and set aside.

Meanwhile, roast the peppers and onions for 25 minutes, until soft and just starting to brown at the edges. Add the beans and stir to mix well. Then, distribute the collard greens over the beans and vegetables. Using oven mitts, carefully cover the sheet pan tightly with foil and return to the oven. Roast for another 10 minutes. The greens will have wilted and softened in the oven. Uncover the pan, then add the lemon juice and stir well. Add additional salt, pepper, or lemon juice as desired.

Divide the baked millet and vegetable-and-bean mixture among four plates, then serve. Both the millet and the vegetable-and-bean mixture will keep in separate airtight containers in the fridge for up to 5 days.

FARRO, SHAVED BRUSSELS SPROUTS, AND NAVY BEANS WITH ALMONDS, DATES, AND DIJON VINAIGRETTE

Makes 4 servings

Grain: farro
Green: brussels sprouts
Bean: navy beans

———————

Think of this as an oven-baked grain salad. Shaved brussels sprouts are roasted until they're crispy, and pearled farro is baked until chewy and tender. These components are tossed together with a mustardy dressing, as well as chopped dates, crunchy roasted almonds, navy beans, and radicchio. The salad has lots of textural complexity and a festive look. I love serving it at holiday gatherings!

To shave the brussels sprouts, you can use a food processor fitted with an S blade, a sharp knife, or a mandoline—or you can find bags of shaved brussels sprouts at many grocery stores.

3 cups / 720ml water

¼ teaspoon and ¼ teaspoon salt, divided, plus extra as needed

1 cup / 180g pearled farro

1 pound / 450g brussels sprouts, ends trimmed, then shaved (see headnote)

1½ tablespoons avocado oil

Freshly ground black pepper

¼ cup / 60ml olive oil

2 tablespoons apple cider vinegar, or more as needed

1 tablespoon Dijon mustard

1 garlic clove, finely minced or grated

1½ cups / 240g cooked navy beans, or 1 (15-ounce / 425g) can navy beans, drained

⅓ cup / 40g roughly chopped roasted and salted almonds

½ cup / 70g chopped pitted Medjool dates

2 cups / 110g packed thinly sliced radicchio

Preheat the oven to 400°F / 200°C.

Bring the water and the ¼ teaspoon salt to a boil in a medium saucepan (or microwave in a microwave-safe liquid measuring cup on high for 4 to 5 minutes). Place the farro in an 8-inch / 20cm square baking pan. Pour the hot water over the farro and cover the pan tightly with foil.

Arrange the brussels sprouts in a single layer on a sheet pan. Drizzle them with the avocado oil and sprinkle with a little salt and pepper. Mix the brussels sprouts to coat with the oil and seasonings.

Place the baking pan with the farro and the sheet pan with the sprouts in the oven. After 10 minutes of roasting, stir the sprouts, then continue baking for another 5 minutes, until the leaves are crisping and are tender. Remove from the oven and set aside.

Bake the farro for 40 minutes, until it has absorbed all the liquid and is plump and tender. If there is any remaining liquid in the baking pan, gently drain it from the grains. Set aside.

For the dressing, whisk together the olive oil, vinegar, mustard, garlic, and remaining ¼ teaspoon salt in a small bowl.

Transfer the farro, the roasted sprouts, and the navy beans, almonds, dates, and radicchio to a large bowl. Pour the dressing over the ingredients and toss the mixture well to incorporate. Taste the grain salad and season as needed with additional salt, pepper, and vinegar. Serve at once. The salad can be stored in an airtight container in the fridge for up to 4 days.

Makes 4 servings

Grain: farro
Green: brussels sprouts
Bean: tempeh

───────

1 (8-ounce / 225g) block tempeh, cut into 1¼-inch / 3cm cubes

2 tablespoons Bragg Liquid Aminos or tamari

1 tablespoon and 1½ tablespoons avocado oil, divided

¼ cup / 60ml freshly squeezed lemon juice

2 teaspoons pure maple syrup or agave nectar

½ teaspoon onion powder

¼ teaspoon smoked paprika

Freshly ground black pepper

12 ounces / 340g brussels sprouts, halved lengthwise, if large

1 large or 2 small sweet potatoes, unpeeled, cut into 1¼-inch / 3cm cubes

Salt

MUSTARD TAHINI DRESSING

2 tablespoons tahini

1½ tablespoons apple cider vinegar

1 tablespoon Dijon mustard

1 tablespoon Bragg Liquid Aminos

2 teaspoons pure maple syrup

1 garlic clove, minced or grated

1 to 2 tablespoons water

4 cups / 640g cooked farro (or a whole grain of choice)

Few handfuls fresh baby greens, such as baby arugula or spinach (optional)

TEMPEH, ROASTED SWEET POTATOES, AND BRUSSELS SPROUTS

I've always loved serving sweet potato and tempeh side by side. One is savory and earthy, the other deeply sweet; one is firm and textured, the other tender. This recipe shows off those contrasts, and it brings crispy roasted brussels sprouts—the green—into the mix.

Place the tempeh cubes in a single or doubled layer in a rectangular storage container with an airtight lid. In a small bowl or liquid measuring cup, whisk together the liquid aminos, 1 tablespoon of the avocado oil, the lemon juice, maple syrup, onion powder, paprika, and ¼ teaspoon black pepper. Pour this marinade over the tempeh. Cover the container tightly and shake a little to disperse the marinade. Place in the fridge and marinate the tempeh for at least 2 hours and up to overnight.

Preheat the oven to 425°F / 220°C. Line two sheet pans with aluminum foil or parchment paper or use nonstick sheet pans.

Remove the tempeh from its marinade and arrange on one sheet pan, reserving the marinade. Place the sprouts and sweet potatoes on the other sheet pan. Drizzle the remaining 1½ tablespoons avocado oil over the vegetables, along with a generous sprinkle of salt and pepper. Stir to coat the vegetables with the seasoning.

Place both sheet pans in the oven. After 8 minutes, flip the tempeh cubes over, brush them with the reserved marinade, then return the tempeh to the oven. Roast the tempeh for another 5 to 7 minutes, until browning, then remove it from the oven and set aside. Roast the vegetables for 15 minutes, then stir them again and bake for 5 to 7 more minutes, until the sweet potatoes are tender and golden at the edges and the brussels sprouts are browning and crispy.

Prepare the dressing. In a small bowl, whisk together the tahini, vinegar, mustard, liquid aminos, maple syrup, and garlic. Whisk in the water, a tablespoon at a time, until it has the consistency you like.

Warm the farro in the microwave or oven if you wish, or serve it cold. Divide the cooked farro among four plates or bowls. Add a handful of baby greens (if using) for color and extra nutrition. Divide the roasted vegetables and tempeh cubes over the grains and greens. Drizzle everything with the sauce and enjoy. The roasted tempeh, vegetables, and sauce can be stored individually in airtight containers in the fridge for up to 5 days.

Makes 4 to 6 servings

Grain: arborio rice
Green: dark leafy green
Bean: edamame

---

2 tablespoons olive oil

1 small or ½ medium white or yellow onion, chopped

2 garlic cloves, minced

8 ounces / 225g sliced fresh shiitake, baby bella, button, oyster, maitake, or mixed mushrooms

½ cup / 120ml dry white wine (or additional broth)

1½ cups / 270g Arborio rice

4 cups / 950ml vegan chicken-style broth or vegetable broth

¼ teaspoon salt

1 tablespoon white miso

2 tablespoons water

2 tablespoons freshly squeezed lemon juice

1 cup / 150g frozen shelled edamame, thawed

3 cups / 60g trimmed and chopped dark leafy greens (such as Swiss chard, curly or Tuscan kale, spinach, or broccoli rabe)

Freshly ground black pepper

Cheesy Topping (page 209), for serving

BAKED RISOTTO WITH MUSHROOMS AND EDAMAME

This risotto starts on the stovetop, gets transferred to the oven for most of its cooking time, and then finishes on the stovetop again. Moving your pot from one place to another may be an unusual cooking method, but it will free your hands from continual stirring and put every minute of the cooking process to good use. The bean in this recipe is shelled edamame—yes, edamame! While it may not be a traditional addition to risotto, it's texturally perfect. Other beans are so soft they might seem to melt into the rice, but the firm little edamame are able to hold their own.

Preheat the oven to 350°F / 175°C.

In a large, oven-safe, heavy-bottomed pot with a lid, heat the olive oil over medium heat. Sauté the onion for 4 to 5 minutes, stirring often, until soft and translucent. Add the garlic and mushrooms, and continue cooking, stirring often, for 6 to 7 minutes, until the mushrooms have released their juices and are tender and reduced in size.

Meanwhile, heat the broth in a heatproof liquid measuring cup in the microwave on high for 4 to 5 minutes or in a saucepan on the stovetop until just at a simmer.

Add the wine to the pot and stir the mushrooms well. Allow the wine to simmer, uncovered, for 5 minutes, to loosen any browned bits, until nearly all the liquid has evaporated. Add the Arborio rice to the pot.

Pour the hot broth into the risotto and add the salt. Stir and cover the pot, then place in the oven. Bake the risotto for 25 to 30 minutes, until the rice has absorbed nearly all the broth. The rice will still be a little al dente at this point, and the risotto will look a little brothy, which is intentional. (If the rice is still uncooked, leave the pot in the oven for another 5 minutes.)

Return the pot to the stovetop. In a small bowl, whisk the miso with the water. Add this mixture, along with the lemon juice, edamame, and greens, to the risotto. Return the risotto to a simmer over medium-low heat and simmer, uncovered, for 5 to 10 more minutes, stirring occasionally, until the greens are tender and the risotto is creamy. Taste the risotto and add freshly ground black pepper to your liking. I like this risotto a little thicker and fluffier than is traditional, but you can adjust the consistency with additional water, if desired.

Divide the risotto among four plates or bowls. Top each portion with some Cheesy Topping and enjoy. Leftover risotto can be stored in an airtight container in the fridge for up to 5 days and can be frozen for up to 6 weeks. Reheat portions of the risotto in a saucepan, adding a splash of water to loosen it up, if necessary.

SHEET-PAN PANZANELLA
WITH ESCAROLE, BURST TOMATOES, AND WHITE BEANS

Makes 4 servings

Grain: bread
Green: escarole
Bean: white beans

Traditional panzanella is one of my favorite things, but much of its success hinges on the perfect ripeness of in-season summer tomatoes. This is a warm version you can make any time of year. Grape or cherry tomatoes turn juicy and sweet through roasting, and hunks of toasted bread become the perfect sponge for soaking them up. The green component is roasted escarole, which takes on a subtle sweetness as it cooks, and the beans are creamy white beans. The texture of your bread is important for this dish: it should be toasted at the edges, but not as crisp or dry as croutons. This will ensure the bread absorbs the vinaigrette, as it's meant to, but doesn't turn to mush once the ingredients are mixed.

Preheat the oven to 400°F / 200°C.

Arrange the escarole and tomatoes on a sheet pan. Drizzle with 2 tablespoons of the olive oil and sprinkle with a pinch of salt. Cover the sheet pan with a loose tent of foil and place in the oven. Roast for 20 minutes, until the escarole is tender and the tomatoes are starting to burst.

Meanwhile, spread the bread cubes on a sheet pan.

Uncover and stir the vegetables, then return to the oven, along with the sheet pan of bread cubes. Roast both for another 10 minutes, until the bread is crisping but not browning and the vegetables are juicy and reduced in size.

Transfer the roasted vegetables and toasted bread to a large bowl. Add the beans.

In a small bowl, whisk together the remaining 3 tablespoons olive oil, the vinegar, shallot, garlic, and ¼ teaspoon salt. Pour the dressing over the salad. Taste and add pepper as needed. Adjust the vinegar and salt to taste. Add an extra drizzle of olive oil and a handful of the parsley (if using). Serve at once. The salad can be stored in an airtight container in the fridge for up to 3 days.

1 small head escarole, core and stem removed, roughly chopped

12 ounces / 340g ripe grape or cherry tomatoes

2 tablespoons and 3 tablespoons olive oil, divided, plus more as needed

Salt

1 (1-pound / 450g) loaf Italian, French, peasant, or sourdough bread, cut or torn into 1½-inch / 4cm pieces

1½ cups cooked cannellini beans, or 1 (15-ounce / 425g) can cannellini beans, drained and rinsed

2 tablespoons red wine vinegar, or more as needed

2 tablespoons finely chopped shallot

1 garlic clove, minced

Freshly ground black pepper

Roughly chopped Italian parsley, for serving (optional)

Makes 6 servings

Grain: bulgur wheat
Green: green cabbage
Bean: black lentils

————————

1 tablespoon olive oil

1 large white or yellow onion, chopped

1½ teaspoons ground cumin

¾ cup / 150g black lentils

4½ cups / 1.07L water

1 cup / 180g bulgur wheat

½ teaspoon fine sea salt, plus more as needed

1 small head green cabbage, trimmed so bottom of cabbage is flat

1 batch (2 cups / 480ml) Red Pepper Sauce (page 214)

CABBAGE BULGUR LENTIL BAKE
WITH RED PEPPER SAUCE

You can think of this dish as a deconstructed version of stuffed cabbage. Rather than stuffing cabbage leaves with filling, I arrange them in a baking pan with alternating layers of smoky red pepper sauce and cumin-scented bulgur wheat and lentils. My favorite way to ready the cabbage leaves for layering and baking is to boil a small head of cabbage whole; it's so easy to then cut the tender leaves off the head. And if you have leaves close to the heart of the cabbage that are too small to use in the bake, you can chop them roughly and add them to your next stir-fry or grain bowl.

In a heavy-bottomed large pot, heat the olive oil over medium heat. Add the onion and sauté, stirring frequently, for 8 to 10 minutes, until tender and starting to brown. Stir in the cumin. Add the lentils to the pot, along with the water. Bring the mixture to a boil, then turn the heat to low. Cover the pot and simmer the lentils for 15 minutes.

Add the bulgur wheat and the ½ teaspoon salt to the pot and stir the ingredients. When the liquid comes to a simmer again, re-cover the pot and cook the lentils and bulgur for 20 more minutes, until the liquid has been absorbed, the bulgur is fluffy, and the lentils are tender. (If the mixture dries out at any point, you can add water by the ¼ cup / 60ml measure to the pot.)

Meanwhile, bring another large pot of water to a boil over medium-high heat. Place the cabbage in the pot, cover, and turn the heat to low. Simmer the cabbage head for 20 to 30 minutes, until it can be pierced easily with a knife. Then drain the cabbage and, using potholders, transfer to a work surface. Allow it to cool for 10 minutes.

Slice the leaves off the head of cabbage. They should cut smoothly and be easy to remove. It's fine if some leaves tear or are so curved you need to cut them in half. (This is a rustic dish, and the layers won't need to appear perfect!)

Preheat the oven to 375°F / 180°C.

Spread ⅔ cup / 80ml of the Red Pepper Sauce in a thin layer on the bottom of a 9 by 13-inch / 23 by 33cm baking pan. Top this with one-third of the cabbage leaves, arranging them flat in a single layer.

CONTINUED

CABBAGE BULGUR LENTIL BAKE
WITH RED PEPPER SAUCE, CONTINUED

Top the leaves with half the bulgur and lentil mixture, then add one-third of the remaining sauce. Repeat this process with another layer of cabbage leaves, bulgur and lentils, and sauce. Finally, top the pan with the remaining cabbage leaves and spread the last of the sauce over them.

Place the baking pan in the oven and bake for 35 to 45 minutes, until sauce is bubbling and the top has darkened a bit. Allow the pan to cool for 15 minutes before cutting into 6 generous squares. Plate the squares as desired. The baked dish can be stored in an airtight container in the fridge for up to 5 days. The cabbage bake can also be frozen, whole or in individual portions, for up to 6 weeks.

ROASTED VEGETABLE COUSCOUS
WITH SWEET POTATO AND WHITE BEAN FRITTERS

Makes 4 servings

Grain: couscous,
bread crumbs
Green: zucchini, parsley
Bean: white beans

Bean fritters are what I make when I want a vegan protein that's crispy and compact like a burger, yet less of a time commitment. The sweet potato and white bean fritters here have a pleasantly toasted exterior and a tender interior. They feel more fun and special than eating unadorned beans, but they won't require you to pile upward of twenty ingredients into your food processor. My favorite way to serve them is with a colorful, jeweled couscous that's packed with roasted vegetables and a generous amount of Tahini Sauce for drizzling and dipping.

Preheat the oven to 400°F / 200°C. Line a sheet pan with aluminum foil.

Place the red onion, zucchini, carrots, and bell peppers on the prepared sheet pan. Drizzle the vegetables with the 2 tablespoons of avocado oil and sprinkle with salt and pepper. Roast the vegetables for 25 to 30 minutes, until tender and browning, stirring halfway through baking.

Meanwhile, bring the water, 2 teaspoons avocado oil, and ¼ teaspoon salt to a boil in a medium pot over medium-high heat. Add the couscous, stir, and cover. Remove the pot from the heat and allow to stand for 5 minutes. Uncover the couscous and fluff lightly with a fork.

Place the couscous in a large bowl and add the roasted vegetables. Drizzle in the vinegar to taste. Set aside.

Prepare the fritters. Line another sheet pan with aluminum foil or use a nonstick sheet pan.

Place the beans in a medium bowl. Cut open the baked sweet potato and measure out ¾ cup / 150g of cooked pulp and add to the bowl. Use a handheld potato masher or fork to mash the beans and sweet potato fairly well; it's okay if some of the beans are only partially smashed. Add the flaxseed, coriander, paprika, garlic powder, salt, and bread crumbs. Mix well, then allow the mixture to rest for 5 minutes; this will help to firm it up.

Use your hands to shape the fritter mixture into eight 2-inch / 5cm balls, then flatten the balls gently to form patties. Brush the foil on the sheet pan with a light layer of avocado oil, then arrange the patties on

1 small red onion, cut into 1-inch / 2.5cm pieces

1 zucchini, quartered lengthwise and cut into 1-inch / 2.5cm pieces

2 carrots, scrubbed, trimmed, halved lengthwise, and cut into 1-inch / 2.5cm pieces

2 bell peppers, any color, cored, seeded, and cut into 1-inch / 2.5cm pieces

2 tablespoons and 2 teaspoons avocado oil, divided

Salt and freshly ground black pepper

1 cup / 240ml water

¾ cup / 170g couscous

1 to 2 tablespoons red wine vinegar

FRITTERS

1½ cups / 280g cooked Great Northern or cannellini beans, or 1 (14.5-ounce / 415g) can cannellini beans, drained (but not rinsed)

1 sweet potato, scrubbed, pricked with a fork, and baked in the microwave or oven until tender

1 tablespoon ground flaxseed

1 teaspoon ground coriander

½ teaspoon smoked paprika

½ teaspoon garlic powder

½ teaspoon salt

CONTINUED

ROASTED VEGETABLE COUSCOUS WITH SWEET
POTATO AND WHITE BEAN FRITTERS, CONTINUED

¼ cup / 30g plain bread crumbs

Avocado oil, for brushing

½ cup / 20g chopped fresh parsley

¾ cup / 180ml Tahini Sauce (page 214)

the sheet. Brush the tops of the patties lightly with oil (or use avocado oil spray). Bake the patties for 10 minutes, then flip and bake for another 8 to 12 minutes, until both sides are golden brown and crispy.

To serve, divide the couscous among four plates. Add two baked fritters to each plate. Garnish the plates with the parsley and drizzle each plate with 2 to 3 tablespoons Tahini Sauce. Serve. The couscous, patties, and sauce can be stored in individual airtight containers in the fridge for up to 5 days.

Makes 6 servings

Grain: quinoa, corn
or wheat tortillas
Green: green cabbage
Bean: tempeh

---

1 (8-ounce / 225g) block
tempeh, crumbled into
small pieces

1 cup / 240ml vegetable
broth, plus more for cooking
the quinoa

¼ cup freshly squeezed
lime juice

2 tablespoons soy sauce

½ teaspoon smoked paprika

½ teaspoon ground cumin

¼ teaspoon garlic powder

1 tablespoon avocado oil

1 red onion, chopped

1 cup / 180g quinoa, rinsed
through a fine-mesh strainer

12 (6-inch / 15cm) corn or
wheat tortillas

SLAW

4 cups / 200g finely shredded
green cabbage

1 cup / 100g shredded carrots

½ small red onion, very thinly
sliced lengthwise, or ½ cup /
65g Quick Pickled Onions
(page 208)

2 tablespoons olive oil

1 tablespoon freshly
squeezed lime juice, or more
as needed

1 tablespoon apple cider
vinegar

1 teaspoon celery seeds
(optional)

¼ teaspoon salt, or more
as needed

TEMPEH QUINOA TACOS
WITH CABBAGE SLAW

Together, small pieces of tempeh and quinoa offer the perfect crumbly texture for a taco filling—not to mention plenty of plant protein. Here, both ingredients get a hands-off preparation with sheet-pan cooking. A fresh, crispy cabbage slaw is the green component, and it adds acidity and crunch to offset the smokiness of the quinoa mixture.

Place the tempeh in a medium container with an airtight lid. Pour the broth over the tempeh, then add the lime juice, soy sauce, paprika, cumin, garlic powder, and avocado oil. Cover the tempeh, shake the container to disperse the marinade, and place in the fridge to marinate for at least 1 hour and up to overnight.

Preheat the oven to 425°F / 220°C. Line a sheet pan with aluminum foil or use a nonstick sheet pan.

Spread the red onion on the prepared sheet pan. Strain the tempeh, reserving the marinade, and add the tempeh to the pan. Spread the tempeh and onion into a thin layer, then place in the oven and bake for 10 minutes. Stir the mixture and continue to bake for another 10 minutes, until the tempeh appears dry and is browning in places.

Pour the reserved marinade into a heatproof liquid measuring cup, then add as much broth (about 1 cup / 240ml) to equal 2 cups / 480ml liquid in total. Warm this mixture in the microwave on high for 3 to 4 minutes, until hot (or heat in a small saucepan until simmering).

Add the quinoa to the sheet pan. Pour the hot liquid over everything in the sheet pan and stir to blend well. Cover the pan tightly with foil, place in the oven, and bake for 20 minutes. Allow the pan to rest for 5 minutes before uncovering the foil. The quinoa will be fully cooked; stir to mix the quinoa, tempeh, and vegetables on the sheet pan.

In the last 5 minutes of baking, wrap the tortillas in foil and place in the oven to get warm. Remove them when you remove the sheet pan.

Prepare the slaw. Place the slaw ingredients in a medium bowl and mix well. Taste the mixture and adjust the salt and lime juice as needed.

To serve, divide the quinoa and tempeh mixture among the warm tortillas and top each tortilla with a small amount of slaw, plus your toppings of choice. The tempeh and quinoa mixture can be stored in an airtight container in the fridge for up to 5 days and frozen for up to 6 weeks. The slaw can be stored in an airtight container for up to 3 days.

½ teaspoon pure maple syrup or agave nectar

¼ cup chopped fresh cilantro (optional)

Cashew Sour Cream (page 216), Guacamole (page 221), Quick Pickled Onions (page 208), or a combination, for serving

Makes 4 servings

Grain: pearl couscous
Green: broccoli
Bean: white beans

———————

2 broccoli crowns, stems peeled, trimmed to 2½ inches / 6.5 cm long

2 tablespoons and 2 teaspoons avocado oil, divided, plus more as needed

Salt and freshly ground black pepper

1 cup / 220g pearl couscous

1¾ cups / 415ml vegetable broth

2 tablespoons harissa paste (mild or spicy)

½ teaspoon ground turmeric

⅓ cup / 25g sliced green onions, green parts only

¼ cup / 40g golden raisins

1 tablespoon freshly squeezed lemon juice

Red pepper flakes (optional)

1 batch (1½ cups / 170g) White Bean Dip (page 220)

Red Pepper Sauce (page 214), Tahini Sauce (page 214), or Green Tahini Sauce (page 216), for drizzling (optional)

BROCCOLI STEAKS WITH WHITE BEAN PUREE AND TURMERIC HARISSA COUSCOUS

You may know and love cauliflower steaks, but what about broccoli steaks? Same idea, different crucifer: broccoli crowns are trimmed and sliced lengthwise to create hearty slabs that feel worthy of a centerpiece on your dinner plate. I always serve vegetable steaks with a grain and a protein source, and in this case, those are harissa-spiced pearl couscous and a bed of creamy white bean dip, respectively. The couscous bakes alongside the broccoli, rather than simmering on the stovetop, so you won't have to divide your attention. If you like, you can finish this dish with a dazzling array of sauce options. This meal is beautiful to look at and feels fancy, despite being relatively easy to prepare. I love serving it to friends.

Preheat the oven to 425°F / 220°C.

Place the broccoli crowns on a work surface and cut each crown vertically into steaks about 1 inch / 2.5cm thick. If your broccoli crowns are small, you may get only two per crown; if bigger, you may end up with 3 or even 4 per crown. These steaks won't be quite as neat or flat as cauliflower steaks tend to be, and that's okay. If they vary a little in size, you'll be able to even out the servings when you serve.

Transfer the steaks to a sheet pan and drizzle the 2 tablespoons avocado oil over them. Use your hands to rub the oil over the steaks to coat on both sides. Make sure that the cut side of each steak is facing down on the sheet pan. Sprinkle the steaks with salt and pepper.

Place the couscous into an 8-inch / 20cm square baking pan. Bring the broth to a boil by microwaving it in a heatproof liquid measuring cup or heating it in a saucepan on the stovetop. Pour the broth over the couscous and stir in the remaining 2 teaspoons avocado oil, the harissa, turmeric, and ¼ teaspoon of salt. Cover the baking pan tightly with foil.

Transfer both the sheet pan and the baking pan to the oven. Roast both for 25 to 30 minutes. The broccoli will be ready when the center of each steak can be pierced with a knife and the edges are browning; the couscous will be ready when all the broth has been absorbed. Remove both from the oven.

Uncover the couscous and fluff it with a fork. If the couscous looks a little dry, you can add a drizzle of oil. Add the green onions, raisins, and lemon juice. Taste the couscous and add additional salt as needed and the red pepper flakes if you'd like a little extra heat.

Spread a generous amount of the bean dip in a round shape onto each of four plates. Arrange a broccoli steak on each circle of dip, then add one-fourth of the couscous mixture to each plate. Top with your choice of sauce; and if you have a dressing you'd like to drizzle on top, go for it. The steaks, white bean dip, and couscous will keep in individual airtight containers in the fridge for up to 5 days.

Makes 4 servings

Grain: gnocchi
Green: arugula
Bean: white beans

———————

1 pound / 450g vegan gnocchi

1 small butternut squash, peeled, seeded, and cut into 1-inch / 2.5cm pieces (about 1 pound / 450g)

2 tablespoons olive oil

Salt and freshly ground black pepper

1½ cups / 240g cooked Great Northern beans, or 1 (15-ounce / 425g) can cannellini beans, drained and rinsed

½ cup / 125ml Pesto (page 217), plus more as needed

2 cups / 60g fresh baby arugula

Freshly squeezed lemon juice

SHEET-PAN GNOCCHI, WHITE BEANS, AND ARUGULA WITH ROASTED BUTTERNUT SQUASH

It may be a stretch to call gnocchi a "grain," but these small potato dumplings do typically contain wheat flour! They're also filling and comforting in the same way that grains and grain-based foods can be. Oven-roasting has become the primary, if not the only, way I prepare gnocchi at home. Roasting ensures that the little dumplings will be tender on the inside, yet lightly crisped on the outside, with no risk of mushiness. Gnocchi will steam if you crowd your sheet pan, just as roasted vegetables do, so it's important to give them breathing space on a pan of their own. Once they're finished, you'll toss them with roasted butternut squash, white beans, and arugula, and you'll dress everything with a batch of lemony Pesto. This meal showcases my favorite food season, that time in early fall when fresh herbs are still abundant and winter squashes are popping up everywhere.

Preheat the oven to 400°F / 200°C.

Arrange the gnocchi on a sheet pan and the butternut squash on another sheet pan. Drizzle each with 1 tablespoon of olive oil. Sprinkle the butternut squash with salt and pepper. Mix the gnocchi and squash on their respective sheet pans, so that both are evenly coated with the oil. Place both pans in the oven. Roast the gnocchi for 20 to 30 minutes, until lightly golden, crispy, and tender on the inside. Roast the squash for 30 to 35 minutes, until tender and lightly browning. Stir both once halfway through the roasting, so everything cooks evenly.

Pour the roasted gnocchi onto the sheet pan with the squash. Add the beans and stir well. Drizzle the ingredients with the pesto, then spread the baby arugula on top. Gently fold in the arugula until everything is coated with pesto. Finish by giving the arugula, gnocchi, squash, and beans a squeeze of lemon juice.

Divide the mixture among four plates or bowls and serve. Store the mixed squash, beans, gnocchi, and arugula in an airtight container in the fridge for up to 4 days.

Makes 4 servings

Grain: quinoa
Green: asparagus
Bean: butter beans

———————

10 large garlic cloves, peeled

1 pound / 450g white or red new potatoes, halved

1 pound / 450g radishes, stemmed, trimmed, and halved

1 tablespoon and ½ tablespoon avocado oil, divided

Coarse salt and freshly ground black pepper

2 cups / 480ml vegetable broth

1 cup / 180g white quinoa, rinsed

1 bunch fresh asparagus, thick ends trimmed, cut into 3-inch / 7.5cm pieces

⅓ cup / 80ml olive oil

¼ cup / 60ml freshly squeezed lemon juice

1 tablespoon apple cider vinegar

2 teaspoons Dijon mustard

½ teaspoon pure maple syrup or agave nectar

¾ teaspoon fine sea salt

1½ cups / 280g cooked butter beans, or 1 (14.5-ounce / 418g) can butter beans, drained and rinsed

Chopped fresh parsley and/ or snipped fresh chives, for serving

BAKED QUINOA, ROASTED SPRING VEGETABLES, AND BUTTER BEANS
WITH ROASTED GARLIC DRESSING

Roasted radishes are so unlike their raw, peppery counterparts; they become tender and their bitterness is mellowed by a subtle sweetness. This dish celebrates roasted radishes, along with asparagus—the green—and creamy new potatoes. You'll put ten of the plumpest garlic cloves you have on your sheet pan and roast them, along with these vegetables. You'll then blend the garlic into a surprisingly savory and intense lemon vinaigrette—the flavorful finishing touch on this light, springtime sheet-pan meal.

Preheat the oven to 400°F / 200°C. Line a sheet pan with aluminum foil or use a nonstick sheet pan.

Arrange the garlic, potatoes, and radishes in a single layer on the sheet pan. Drizzle the vegetables with 1 tablespoon of avocado oil and sprinkle them with coarse salt and pepper. Mix the vegetables to coat them evenly with the oil.

In a medium saucepan, bring the broth to a boil. (Alternatively, place the broth in a heatproof liquid measuring cup and microwave on high for 3 to 4 minutes, until very hot.) Place the quinoa in an 8-inch / 20cm square baking pan. Pour the broth over the quinoa, then cover the baking pan tightly with foil.

Place the sheet pan and baking pan in the oven. After 25 minutes, remove the baking pan. Allow to stand, still covered, for 5 minutes, then lightly fluff the grains with a fork. The quinoa should have absorbed all the liquid; re-cover it and set it aside.

Roast the potatoes, radishes, and garlic on the sheet pan for 10 minutes, then stir them and continue to roast for another 15 minutes. Stir again and push the vegetables to one side of the sheet pan. Add the asparagus pieces to the other side and drizzle the asparagus with the remaining ½ tablespoon avocado oil. Sprinkle with coarse salt and pepper, then return the sheet pan to the oven to roast for another 15 to 20 minutes, until the radishes are tender, the potatoes are browning, and the asparagus is crisp-tender.

Using a spoon or tongs, pick out the garlic cloves and place them in a food processor or blender. Add the olive oil, lemon juice, vinegar, mustard, maple syrup, sea salt, and a generous pinch of pepper. Blend for 1 minute, until very smooth.

Add the butter beans to the sheet pan with the vegetables and stir well. To serve, divide the quinoa among four plates or bowls. Top each serving with one-fourth of the vegetable mixture, then drizzle the plates with a couple tablespoons of the dressing and garnish with the parsley. The vegetables and quinoa can be stored separately in airtight containers in the fridge for up to 4 days. The vinaigrette can be stored in an airtight container or jar for up to 1 week.

If there's anything that food blogging has taught me, it's that no recipe is too basic to write about. For example, I always hesitate before I publish a simple salad dressing online. But recipes for homemade dressings and other condiments inevitably generate lots of questions and comments, which indicates to me that there's a real need for them.

If we judge a recipe by its usefulness, the following basic recipes might be the most important ones in this book. These sauces, dressings, dips, and toppings can spell the difference between a recipe that's good and a recipe that's outstanding.

For instance, no matter how tasty one of my pasta recipes is, I can all but guarantee that it's better with my Cheesy Topping (page 209), a savory mixture of nutritional yeast, cashews, and salt. I wouldn't want to eat my Stuffed Bell Peppers (page 165) without big spoonfuls of Guacamole (page 221). And my dairy-free life would be infinitely harder without the creamy texture offered to me by Cashew Sour Cream (page 216).

These basic recipes also include some simple proteins. Eggy Tofu (page 212) is marinated and baked slabs of tofu that acquire an eggy flavor, thanks to black salt and nutritional yeast. You can enjoy them in sandwiches, noodle bowls, and more. Cheesy Tofu (page 210), meanwhile, is crumbled and marinated tofu with briny and salty flavors, resulting in a plant-based ingredient reminiscent of feta. It's wonderful in grain salads and pastas, including the Barley, Cheesy Tofu, and Cucumber with Sungold Tomatoes (page 40) and the Quinoa, Crumbled Cheesy Tofu, Roasted Corn, and Romaine (page 53).

Once you get to know these sauces, dressings, and dips, you'll start finding all the many possibilities for using them. The recipes in this cookbook are only a starting point.

BASICS

Makes 2 cups / 260g

QUICK PICKLED ONIONS

½ cup / 120ml water

⅓ cup / 80ml apple cider vinegar or white wine vinegar

1 teaspoon salt

1½ teaspoons sugar

1 red onion, thinly sliced

Quick Pickled Onions are assertive, just as raw onions are, but they're also a little more mellow. What they lose in spiciness is replaced by acid, which I love. Pickled onions add vibrancy and character to a dish in an instant, and you'll see that I rely on them often to elevate otherwise simple recipes, including a mashup of Pasta and Three Beans salad (page 61), a refreshing sandwich with black beans, cucumber, and avocado (see page 102), and a wilted kale salad with farro and lentils (see page 68).

In a small saucepan, bring the water and vinegar to a simmer over medium-high heat. (Alternatively, microwave the liquid in a heatproof liquid measuring cup for 2 minutes on high.) Stir in the salt and sugar.

Place the sliced onion in a pint-sized mason jar, preferably wide-mouth, that will hold the onion with an inch of headspace. Pour the hot vinegar mixture over the onion and use a spoon to press the slices down into the hot liquid. Cover the jar. Allow it to cool for 30 minutes at room temperature, then transfer it to the fridge for storage. The pickled onion will keep in an airtight container in the fridge for up to 4 weeks.

CHEESY TOPPING

½ cup / 70g unsalted raw whole cashews

⅓ cup / 20g nutritional yeast

½ teaspoon fine sea salt

You can't love pasta as much as I do without craving the salty, umami-rich parmesan cheese that serves as a standard finishing touch—or more—in classic Italian recipes. This simple mixture of cashews, nutritional yeast, and salt does the (vegan) trick! Together, the three ingredients instantly add savoriness and texture to any dish that could use a boost.

Place the cashews, nutritional yeast, and salt in a food processor fitted with the S blade and process until finely ground. The cashews should be broken down, but not quite powdery. The topping can be stored in an airtight container in the fridge for up to 4 weeks.

CRISPY CHICKPEAS

Makes 1½ cups / 140g

1½ cups / 240g cooked chickpeas, or 1 (15-ounce / 425g) can chickpeas, drained and rinsed

1½ tablespoons avocado oil

½ teaspoon fine sea salt

¼ teaspoon onion powder

¼ teaspoon garlic powder

Freshly ground black pepper

Think crispy, crunchy, crouton-like energy, but with the nutritional goodness of legumes: that's what roasted chickpeas can offer in any dish. I use them to top salads, bowls, and soups, adding crunch where needed, and to snack on by the handful.

Preheat the oven to 400°F / 200°C.

Spread the chickpeas on a sheet pan and use tea towels or paper towels to roll them around and pat them dry. The drier the chickpeas, the crispier they'll be. Also make sure there's no liquid remaining on the sheet pan; use paper towels to wipe it up.

Drizzle the chickpeas with the oil and use your hands or a spoon to coat them evenly. Sprinkle them with the salt, onion powder, garlic powder, and a few turns of black pepper. Mix again.

Place the sheet pan in the oven and roast the chickpeas, stirring them once halfway through, until they're a deep golden brown and very crispy, 25 to 35 minutes. The chickpeas can be used immediately or stored in an airtight container for up to 5 days in the fridge. Enjoy them as a snack at room temperature or reheat in a 300°F / 150°C oven for about 15 minutes.

Makes 10 slices or 3 cups /
550g crumbled (enough for
4 servings)

CHEESY TOFU

1 (14-ounce / 400g) block
extra-firm or firm tofu,
pressed (see page 212)

3 tablespoons white miso

2 tablespoons nutritional
yeast

¼ teaspoon salt

¼ cup / 60ml freshly
squeezed lemon juice

2 teaspoons red wine vinegar

2 tablespoons water

There's an abundance of commercial plant-based cheese available in stores now, but it's empowering to have a simple, unfussy homemade alternative. When extra-firm tofu is marinated in a mixture of white miso, lemon juice, and nutritional yeast, it takes on a tangy, salty flavor that's reminiscent of cheese. You can cut the tofu into slabs and layer it in sandwiches, as you might layer slices of mozzarella; that's the idea in my Tofu, Pesto, and Tomato Caprese (page 97). You can also use it as a briny ingredient reminiscent of feta. If you do that, you have the choice of crumbling it, as I suggest for the Quinoa, Crumbled Cheesy Tofu, Roasted Corn, and Romaine salad (page 53). You can also dice it, as I do in my Beet Couscous, Cheesy Tofu, Green Beans, and Watercress salad (page 33) and in the Barley, Cheesy Tofu, and Cucumber with Sungold Tomatoes (page 40). Once you get into the habit of having this marinated tofu in the fridge, you'll see how versatile it can be.

Choose the best option for your intended use. If preparing slabs, then cut the tofu crosswise into ⅜-inch / 1cm slices and place the slices in a rectangular airtight storage container. If you'd like the crumbed version (so that the tofu resembles feta), crumble it into the container instead of layering it. For small cubes, dice the tofu into ¼-inch / 6mm cubes, then place them in the container.

In a small bowl or liquid measuring cup, whisk together the miso, nutritional yeast, salt, lemon juice, and vinegar until smooth. Add the water and whisk again. Pour this mixture over the tofu, cover the container, shake it gently to disperse the marinade, and place it in the fridge to marinate overnight. The marinated tofu will keep for up to 5 days in an airtight container in the fridge.

EGGY TOFU

1 (16-ounce / 450g) block super-firm tofu (see headnote)

½ teaspoon ground turmeric

½ teaspoon kala namak (Himalayan black salt) or fine sea salt

1½ tablespoons nutritional yeast

2 teaspoons avocado oil, or more as needed

Freshly ground black pepper

So many grain bowls, toasts, and salad recipes give the option of topping whatever is being served with a fried or soft-boiled egg. If you prepare a batch of these golden-hued slabs of tofu, they can be as convenient and versatile a protein as the proverbial "egg on top." To season the tofu here, I use black salt and nutritional yeast, which create an eggy flavor, as well as turmeric, which turns the tofu golden. If you can find tofu that's labeled "super-firm," or "high protein," I recommend using it, as its sturdy consistency holds up well to pan-frying. Otherwise, extra-firm tofu will get the job done. Use this tofu in the Cold Kimchi Noodles (page 65), in a breakfast English muffin dish (see page 86), or as a means of making any grain, green, and bean meal even more nutritious.

Slice the tofu crosswise into ¼-inch / 6mm slices for a total of 8 to 10 slices. Pat the slices dry. In a small bowl, mix the turmeric, kala namak, and nutritional yeast.

Heat the avocado oil in a large skillet over medium heat. Add the tofu slices in a single layer; you may need to do this in two batches. Sprinkle the spice mixture over the slices until evenly covered, then add a turn or two of freshly ground black pepper. After 2 to 3 minutes, or when the bottom sides of the tofu are just browning, flip the slices over. Sprinkle the new tops with the spice mixture and a turn or two of pepper. After 2 minutes, flip the tofu slices over again, allow them to cook for 1 more minute, then transfer to a plate.

Cook the remaining slices, adding avocado oil to the skillet as needed. The tofu slices can be stored in an airtight container in the fridge for up to 5 days.

SAVORY SOY CURLS

Makes 3 cups / 180g (enough for 4 servings)

4 ounces / 120g soy curls (½ standard bag of Butler Foods soy curls)

½ teaspoon smoked paprika

2 tablespoons nutritional yeast

3 cups / 720ml vegetable broth

1 tablespoon Bragg Liquid Aminos

Because beans are such a primary focus in this book, I chose not to include many vegan meats. Yet, here's a recipe that rivals the best vegan "chicken" in grocery stores, and it is, in fact, a bean! The soy curls produced by Butler Foods contain only one ingredient—whole, non-GMO soybeans. These soybeans have been puffed and dehydrated, and when you rehydrate them in hot, seasoned liquid, you get a versatile protein reminiscent of the texture of chicken.

After rehydrating soy curls, I often bake them for a slightly crispy texture. I love to then use them in stir-fry dishes, sandwiches and wraps, and sheet-pan meals such as the Sheet-Pan Shawarma-Spiced Soy Curls (page 179).

Preheat the oven to 425°F / 220°C. Line a sheet pan with parchment paper or use a nonstick sheet.

Place the soy curls in a large bowl and toss with the paprika and nutritional yeast.

In a medium pot, bring the broth and liquid aminos to a boil over medium-high heat. Pour the liquid over the soy curls, cover the bowl, and allow the curls to hydrate for 10 minutes.

Drain the soy curls through a colander or large strainer. Use the bottom of a bowl to press down on the soy curls in the strainer, ensuring that as much marinade as possible is drained off.

Spread the soy curls on the prepared sheet pan and bake for 10 minutes. Stir the soy curls, then continue to bake for another 5 to 10 minutes, until the soy curls are just starting to brown. They should be moist in the center but have some crispiness at the edges. The soy curls can be stored in an airtight container in the fridge for up to 5 days or frozen for up to 6 weeks.

RED PEPPER SAUCE

Makes 2 cups / 480ml

1 (16-ounce / 450g) jar roasted red peppers, drained

¼ cup / 60ml olive oil

2 tablespoons white wine vinegar

1 garlic clove, roughly chopped

1 teaspoon smoked paprika

¼ teaspoon salt

2 tablespoons roughly chopped shallot or red onion

2 teaspoons pure maple syrup

I can't think of a harder working pantry item than a jar of roasted red peppers. Simultaneously tangy, salty, briny, and sweet, marinated and roasted red peppers add concentrated flavor to pasta, salads, or pilafs in an instant. They also can be used to make this creamy sauce, which is ubiquitous in my home. Pour the sauce onto a plate of warm Turmeric Rice (page 143), use it to simmer some plump butter beans (see page 93), or mix it with pasta as a refreshing alternative to marinara sauce. The possibilities are endless!

Place all the ingredients in a blender or food processor. Blend for 2 to 3 minutes, until the sauce is smooth. The sauce can be stored in an airtight container in the fridge for up to 1 week or frozen for up to 6 weeks.

TAHINI SAUCE

Makes ¾ cup / 180ml

6 tablespoons / 90g tahini

2½ tablespoons freshly squeezed lemon juice

6 tablespoons / 90ml water

½ teaspoon fine sea salt

1 garlic clove, minced or finely grated

Tahini is my favorite base for making creamy sauces; in fact, I could probably produce a small ebook of all the tahini dressings I've made over the years. Most of the time, however, I come back to one simple, tried-and-true formula: tahini, water, lemon, salt, and garlic.

In a small bowl or liquid measuring cup, whisk together the tahini, lemon juice, and 2 tablespoons of the water. The tahini will seize up a bit; add another 2 tablespoons of water and whisk again. At this point, you should have a thick, smooth mixture. Add the final 2 tablespoons of water and whisk again until smooth. Then, stir in the salt and garlic. Taste and adjust the salt to your liking. Store the sauce in an airtight container in the fridge for up to 1 week.

GREEN TAHINI SAUCE

Makes ¾ cup / 180ml

6 tablespoons / 90g tahini

2½ tablespoons freshly squeezed lemon juice

½ cup / 120ml water, or more as needed

½ teaspoon fine sea salt

1 garlic clove, minced or finely grated

⅓ cup / 7g tightly packed fresh parsley

⅓ cup / 7g tightly packed fresh basil

4 green onions, green parts only, roughly chopped

This version of tahini sauce has a bright green color and herbaceous flavor, thanks to the addition of parsley, basil, and green onion tops. Think of it as a hybrid of tahini and green goddess dressings, and don't be afraid to get playful with the herbs. I've made the sauce with dill, chives, and even cilantro. My favorite use for this dressing is over a big platter of Pita Chips and Crispy Chickpeas with Broccolini (page 81), but I also love to drizzle it over roasted carrots.

Place all the ingredients in a blender or food processor and process until smooth. If the dressing seems too thick, add additional water by the tablespoon. Store the sauce in an airtight container in the fridge for up to 4 days.

CASHEW SOUR CREAM

Makes scant ¾ cup / 225g

¾ cup / 105g raw cashews, soaked for at least 2 hours and drained

1 tablespoon freshly squeezed lemon juice

½ tablespoon freshly squeezed lime juice

½ teaspoon fine sea salt

⅓ cup / 80ml water

No condiment gets more use in my home than cashew cream, a luxurious staple that serves as a multipurpose replacement for dairy. This version contains a good amount of citrus for acidity and a slightly tart flavor, so I'm calling it Cashew Sour Cream. It's also reminiscent of a thick, strained yogurt or crème fraîche. I rely on it whenever a creamy consistency is needed, from pasta dishes to soups, to a vegan spin on egg salad (see page 106).

The recipe can be doubled or tripled; I'm never sorry to have an extra stash on hand.

Place the cashews, lemon and lime juices, salt, and water in a high-speed blender or food processor and process until smooth. If using a food processor, stop once or twice during blending to scrape down the sides of the bowl. Store the sour cream in an airtight container in the fridge for up to 4 days or freeze for up to 6 weeks.

PESTO

I like pesto pasta, but in my mind, pesto is more of an all-purpose condiment than a pasta sauce. I enjoy spreading it onto sandwiches, drizzling it over hot roasted vegetables, and piling it into the center of my grain bowls.

This pesto recipe is my longtime go-to. Here, you blanch the basil before blending it. It's an extra step to be sure, but it keeps the basil a beautiful bright green when stored. Speaking of green, that's another thing I love about this sauce—use it, and you'll automatically add one more green to your meal.

2 cups / 40g tightly packed fresh basil

½ cup / 70g raw cashews

2 garlic cloves, roughly chopped

½ teaspoon fine sea salt, or more as needed

6 tablespoons / 90ml olive oil, or more as needed

3 tablespoons / 45g nutritional yeast

Freshly ground black pepper

1 tablespoon freshly squeezed lemon juice, or more as needed

Bring a medium pot of water to a boil over high heat. While the water is heating up, prepare an ice bath in a medium bowl.

Turn off the heat and add the basil to the hot water. Blanch for 15 seconds, then use a slotted spoon to transfer the basil to the ice bath. By the time you transfer all of it, most of the basil will have blanched for about 30 seconds. Allow the basil to remain in the ice bath for 3 to 5 minutes.

Place a few tea towels or paper towels on your work surface and use the slotted spoon to spread the basil on the towels. Use the towels to press the basil firmly, so you remove all the excess water.

Place the cashews, garlic, and salt in a food processor fitted with the S blade. Add the basil and pulse the ingredients until ground. Run the processor and gradually add the olive oil, pouring it through the spout in a thin stream. Stop the processor and scrape down the sides. Add the nutritional yeast, a few turns of pepper, and the lemon juice. Process the pesto for 1 more minute; it will be on the thick side.

Taste the pesto and adjust the lemon juice, salt, and pepper as needed. If the pesto is too thick for your liking, add a tablespoon or two of olive oil and pulse to combine. The pesto can be stored in an airtight container in the fridge for up to 5 days or frozen for up to 8 weeks.

CHICKPEA HUMMUS

Each time I'm tempted to purchase hummus, I remind myself that in the time it would take me to run to the store, I can easily make hummus at home. I'm almost never without a can of chickpeas, plus the tahini, lemon, and salt that are the base ingredients of this easy recipe. Instead of blending the hummus with olive oil or water, I use aquafaba, or reserved brine from the can. Aquafaba contains starch, and this starch creates a hummus that's especially creamy, smooth, and light.

1 (15-ounce / 425g) can chickpeas, drained but not rinsed, liquid reserved

¼ cup / 60g tahini

2 tablespoons freshly squeezed lemon juice, or more as needed

1 to 2 garlic cloves, or more as needed

1 teaspoon salt, or more as needed

½ teaspoon ground cumin

Pour ¼ cup / 60ml of the canning liquid into a liquid measuring cup and set aside.

Place the chickpeas in a food processor fitted with the S blade. Add the tahini, lemon juice, 1 garlic clove, the salt, and cumin. Pour in 2 tablespoons of the canning liquid. Process the mixture for 3 to 4 minutes, stopping once halfway through to stir the hummus and scrape down the sides of the processor bowl. Stop processing when the hummus is silky smooth and a pale beige color. If the hummus is too thick for your liking, add the remaining 2 tablespoons canning liquid. Taste the hummus, then adjust the salt, garlic, and lemon as needed. The hummus can be stored in an airtight container in the fridge for up to 5 days.

Variation: Red Pepper Hummus
Makes scant 2 cups / 500g

Reserve only 2 tablespoons of the canning liquid when you drain the chickpeas. Add 1 cup / 200g of drained roasted red bell peppers to the chickpeas and other ingredients in the food processor before processing. Process for a few minutes, scrape down the sides of the processor bowl, then decide if you need to add more of the reserved canning liquid; this depends on how thick you like your hummus and how much liquid the roasted peppers added to the mixture. Process until the hummus is silky smooth. The hummus can be stored in an airtight container in the fridge for up to 5 days.

WHITE BEAN DIP

**Makes 1½ cups / 170g
(enough for 4 servings)**

2 garlic cloves

1 (15-ounce / 425g) can
cannellini beans or Great
Northern beans, drained but
not rinsed, liquid reserved

2 tablespoons olive oil

½ teaspoon salt, or more
as needed

2 tablespoons freshly
squeezed lemon juice,
or more as needed

Freshly ground black pepper

Handful of fresh herbs
(such as basil, dill, parsley,
or chives; optional)

This lemony, garlicky dip has an especially creamy quality, thanks
to two things: the inherently buttery texture of cannellini beans
and the canning liquid they're packed in. Reserve ¼ cup / 60ml of
this liquid before you drain the beans entirely, and don't rinse them
before you start processing.

Place the garlic in a food processor fitted with the S blade. Pulse a few
times to roughly chop the garlic.

Reserve ¼ cup / 60ml of the bean canning liquid; if you can't get this
much liquid, add water to reach ¼ cup / 60ml.

Place the beans in a food processor fitted with the S blade. Add the
olive oil, salt, lemon juice, and reserved bean liquid. Process for 2 to
3 minutes, until smooth and creamy, stopping once to scrape down
the sides of the bowl. Taste the dip; adjust the salt and lemon as
desired and add pepper to taste. Add the fresh herbs, if using, to the
processor and pulse a few times to incorporate. The dip will keep in
an airtight container in the fridge for up to 4 days and can be frozen
for up to 6 weeks.

GUACAMOLE

Every person has their own guacamole preferences: chunky or smooth, spicy or mild, lots of onion versus a little, heaps of cilantro, or none at all. This is my Goldilocks recipe. It's tart, salty, and not too spicy. I'll let you decide how chunky you'd like the guacamole to be. My texture preference changes with my mood!

Slice the avocados in half lengthwise and remove the pits. Scoop the flesh into a medium bowl. Use a large fork to roughly mash the avocado. Add the lime juice and salt and continue mashing until the avocados are well mashed, with some texture remaining; you can make it smoother, depending on your preferences.

Fold the red onion and cilantro into the guacamole. Taste the guacamole; adjust the salt and lime juice and add the red pepper flakes as desired. The guacamole can be stored in an airtight container in the fridge with a layer of plastic wrap or a few slices of fresh lemon on top to help prevent the top layer from browning for up to 2 days.

3 ripe Hass avocados

3 tablespoons freshly squeezed lime juice, or more as needed

½ teaspoon salt, or more as needed

½ cup / 70g finely diced red onion

⅓ cup / 15g chopped fresh cilantro

Red pepper flakes (optional)

If this section were titled "Dessert," there would be an array of pies, pastries, tarts, cakes, cookies, and confections. But it's not so titled. The five recipes that follow are "sweet things." These can be desserts, if you want them to be, but they can also be snacks or breakfast treats. Sweet things are comforting and uplifting; I can't promise that a chocolate chunk cookie, a slice of perfectly moist vegan banana bread, or a square of chocolate cake will fix a stressful work situation or eliminate a low mood, but I can all but guarantee they'll leave you a little happier than you were before.

Sweet things include those easy yet impressive treats that come to your rescue when you have friends coming over unexpectedly or a last-minute dinner party to which you don't want to show up empty-handed. In these cases, I highly recommend a piping hot dish of fruit crumble (see page 227). Better yet, I recommend one that's made with frozen fruit, so that it can be prepared at any time of the year—regardless of what's in season and whether you've remembered to shop that week.

If it's one of those days when a traditional and sensible breakfast—oatmeal, avocado toast, whatever—really isn't going to cut it, I can vouch for a tender, citrus-scented slice of Olive Oil Cake (page 231). I like to serve mine with vanilla ice cream, but if that doesn't call to you first thing in the morning, try some yogurt instead.

These recipes are sweet little gifts that you can give to yourself. I've purposely chosen the five treats I love and make most often. This cookbook wasn't originally intended to include sweets, but I told my editor that it felt sad to publish a recipe collection without them.

I stand by those words. I hope that no amount of focus on grains, greens, and beans will keep you from celebrating life's sweetness—on and off the plate.

CHOCOLATE CHUNK COOKIES

1 tablespoon / 8g ground flaxseed

3 tablespoons water

¾ cup / 90g unbleached all-purpose flour

¼ teaspoon salt

¾ teaspoon baking powder

8 tablespoons / 100g lightly packed brown sugar

6 tablespoons / 90g nut or seed butter (peanut, almond, cashew, sunflower seed, sesame seed, etc.)

½ teaspoon vanilla extract

3 ounces / 90g / ⅔ cup vegan dark chocolate, roughly chopped

Flaky salt, such as Maldon, for topping

We all need a go-to chocolate chip (or in this case, chocolate chunk) cookie recipe, and this is mine. A while back, fellow recipe blogger Jessie Snyder posted a chocolate chip cookie recipe that used almond butter as a fat source. I'm accustomed to making vegan cookies with vegan butter, and I was skeptical that nut butter—an ingredient that can be temperamental in baking—could carry a solid cookie recipe. I should never have doubted Jessie, whose cookies were a resounding success. Through tinkering with them, I've created my own chocolate chunk cookie that uses nut or seed butter as a base.

The beauty of this recipe is that you can make it with pretty much any nut or seed butter. I've tested it with peanut, almond, cashew, and sunflower seed butters, as well as tahini. All versions work. Each has a distinctive taste, thanks to the nut or seed that lends its richness to the cookie. You'll find that the tahini cookies have a slight bitterness; the sunflower seed cookies offer deep, toasty notes; the cashew cookies carry a mild sweetness; and so on. The preparation process for each variation is the same, but precision matters with this recipe, so be sure to follow the instructions carefully and use a scale if you have one.

I like my cookies studded with great big chunks of chocolate, rather than evenly dispersed with chips. Be sure to find a bar of dark chocolate that's vegan; most bars labeled at 60% or higher are!

Preheat the oven to 350°F / 175°C. Line a sheet pan with parchment paper.

Place the flaxseed in a medium bowl. Add the water, stir well, and set aside.

In another medium bowl, whisk together the flour, salt, and baking powder.

Add the brown sugar, nut or seed butter, and vanilla to the bowl with the flaxseed. Whisk thoroughly to combine, until you have an even, wet mixture. Add the dry ingredients. Use a spoon or a spatula to mix well. The resulting cookie dough will be dense, so use some elbow grease with this step. Add the chocolate chunks and mix again, until they're evenly distributed. The dough will have plenty of chocolate in it.

Roll the dough into balls 1¼ to 1½ inches / 3 to 4cm in diameter; you're aiming to get 12 cookies. Arrange the balls on the sheet pan 2 inches / 5cm apart, then press them gently to flatten them just a bit; avoid turning them into pancakes. Sprinkle with the flaky salt.

Place the cookies in the oven and bake for 9 minutes, until puffy. They may look a little pale and underbaked, but they'll continue to bake after you remove them from the oven; timing here is precise. Allow the cookies to cool on the sheet pan for 5 minutes, then very gently use a spatula to transfer them to a wire cooling rack.

Allow the cookies to cool for at least another 15 minutes before enjoying. The cookies can be stored in an airtight container at room temperature for up to 2 days, in the fridge for up to 5 days, or in the freezer for up to 8 weeks.

FROZEN FRUIT CRUMBLE

Knowing that I often forget to eat fresh fruit before it spoils, I keep my freezer stocked with bags of frozen berries, peaches, and cherries. Sometimes I simmer and add them to my morning oatmeal, and sometimes I use them to make this easy, economical fruit crumble.

The proportion of crumble topping to fruit in this recipe is significant, but that's intentional: it means you don't have to toss the fruit filling with flour or sugar as an initial step. Just dump your frozen berries, peaches, or cherries into a baking pan, spritz them with lemon juice, and then distribute the crumble topping over them. The generously portioned topping will soak up liquid from the frozen fruits as they cook and become nicely browned on top. If you keep a bag of frozen fruit around for smoothies, and you have some flour, sugar, and avocado oil in your pantry, then you can whip up this dessert at a moment's notice. A scoop of vegan ice cream, yogurt, or whipped cream would be icing on the proverbial cake.

5 cups / 700g frozen berries (mixed or single variety), pitted cherries or chunked peaches

1½ tablespoons freshly squeezed lemon juice

1¾ cups / 210g unbleached all-purpose flour

½ cup / 100g lightly packed brown sugar

¼ cup / 50g cane sugar

½ teaspoon salt

½ cup / 120ml avocado or olive oil

Vegan ice cream, for serving (optional)

Preheat the oven to 350°F / 175°C. Lightly oil or line an 8-inch / 20cm square baking pan with parchment paper.

Spread the frozen fruit in the baking pan, then drizzle the lemon juice over it.

In a medium bowl, whisk together the flour, sugars, and salt. Pour the avocado oil into the bowl, then use a spoon to mix the ingredients until roughly combined, with a bit of unmixed flour still visible. This won't look like a traditional crumb topping, since you're not working with cold butter. Instead, it will be wet and clumpy, and that's okay! Use your hands or the same spoon to gently distribute the topping over the fruit.

Place the pan in the oven and bake for 50 to 60 minutes, until the fruit is quite crispy and browning on top and the fruit itself is juicy and cooked down. Serve warm, with vegan ice cream, if desired. The crumble can be stored in an airtight container in the fridge for up to 4 days and frozen for up to 6 weeks.

CHOCOLATE SNACK CAKE

1¼ cups / 150g unbleached all-purpose flour

½ cup / 40g Dutch-process unsweetened cocoa powder

½ teaspoon salt

¾ teaspoon baking powder

½ teaspoon baking soda

⅓ cup / 80ml avocado oil

¾ cup / 150g cane sugar

1 teaspoon vanilla extract

1 cup / 240ml water

1 teaspoon apple cider vinegar, lemon juice, or distilled white vinegar

If you ask me, everyone needs a chocolate cake recipe that's not reserved for birthdays or special occasions. Instead, its purpose is to supply a light, moist square of chocolatey goodness at any time of day. Taking inspiration from the Swedish custom of fika, my own favorite way to enjoy squares of this cake is with a sip of afternoon coffee. The cake is intentionally icing free, and I like its simplicity. If you'd like to dress it up a little—for example, if you want to transform it from snack cake to a more formal dessert—then serve it with vegan whipped cream, a dusting of confectioners' sugar, a raspberry coulis or fresh berries, or a scoop of ice cream.

Preheat the oven to 350°F / 175°C. Line the bottom of an 8-inch / 20cm square baking pan with parchment paper. Lightly oil the sides of the pan.

In a large bowl, mix the flour, cocoa powder, salt, baking powder, and baking soda.

In another medium bowl, whisk together the avocado oil, sugar, vanilla, water, and vinegar for a full minute, until the wet ingredients are well combined.

Add the wet ingredients to the dry ingredients and mix fully. Some small clumps are fine, but there should be no large clumps or streaks of flour in the batter. This is a relatively loose/wet batter for cake—that's how it should be!

Pour the batter into the prepared baking pan. Bake the cake for 35 to 40 minutes, until the top of the cake is domed and set. Allow the cake to cool on a wire cooling rack for at least 30 minutes before removing the cake from its pan. Allow the cake to rest on the cooling rack for another 1 to 2 hours, until room temperature, before cutting into nine squares. The cake squares can be stored in an airtight container at room temperature for up to 3 days. They can be frozen for up to 6 weeks.

OLIVE OIL CAKE

I love going out to eat Italian food. While it's never hard for me to find excellent pizza or pasta dishes that are vegan, I'm all too accustomed to gazing at Italian pastries and cakes as they pass by me in restaurants, knowing that they're likely prepared with egg or dairy. Thankfully, there's homemade olive oil cake to console me. I tend to like cakes that are light and fluffy, but olive oil cake should have some richness and density. This is usually achieved with a generous amount of fat in the form of olive oil and egg yolks. Instead, I create it with tahini, which is simultaneously an effective egg replacer and a way to preserve moisture in the cake as it bakes. The cake doesn't require decoration, but I like to serve it with a thin layer of sifted confectioners' sugar on top. Fresh or stewed fruit, vegan whipped cream, and jam are all wonderful accompaniments.

2 cups / 240g unbleached all-purpose flour

½ teaspoon salt

¾ teaspoon baking powder

½ teaspoon baking soda

1 tablespoon grated orange zest

½ cup / 120ml olive oil

¼ cup / 60ml freshly squeezed orange juice

1 cup / 240ml plain soy, oat, almond, or cashew milk

¾ cup / 150g cane sugar

1 teaspoon vanilla extract

½ teaspoon almond extract or orange extract (optional)

2 tablespoons tahini

Confectioners' sugar, for dusting; or jam, fresh fruit, stewed fruit, or vegan whipped cream, for serving (optional)

Preheat the oven to 350°F / 175°C. Line the bottom of a 9-inch / 23cm round baking pan with parchment paper and lightly oil the sides.

In a large bowl, whisk together the flour, salt, baking powder, and baking soda. Stir in the orange zest.

In a medium bowl, whisk together the olive oil, orange juice, non-dairy milk, sugar, vanilla, almond extract (if using), and tahini. When this mixture is relatively smooth, pour it into the bowl with the dry ingredients.

Fold the batter together with a spatula until no streaks of flour are visible. Continue mixing and folding until the batter is relatively smooth; a few small lumps are okay. Pour the batter into the baking pan and bake for 40 minutes, until the top of the cake is domed and golden brown. Allow the cake to cool in the pan on a wire cooling rack for at least 30 minutes before removing the cake from its pan. Allow the cake to rest on the cooling rack for another 1 to 2 hours, until room temperature.

Cut the cake into slices and serve the cake with desired accompaniments or decorations. The cake can be stored in an airtight container at room temperature for up to 3 days. It can be frozen for up to 6 weeks.

BANANA BREAD

½ cup / 120ml soy, oat, almond, or cashew milk

1 tablespoon freshly squeezed lemon juice

2 cups / 240g unbleached all-purpose flour

½ teaspoon baking soda

1 teaspoon baking powder

½ teaspoon salt

½ teaspoon ground cinnamon

½ cup / 120ml avocado oil

¾ cup / 150g packed brown sugar

1 heaping cup / 250g mashed overripe banana (3 medium or 4 small)

1 teaspoon vanilla extract

½ cup / 60g chopped walnuts or chopped vegan dark chocolate (optional)

If I had to choose between the most creative or decadent dessert in the world and a perfect slice of banana bread, I think I'd choose banana bread every time. There's no treat I enjoy more as an afternoon pick-me-up or a sweet breakfast. I've been using the same classic, no-frills recipe for years, sometimes with the addition of chopped walnuts or dark chocolate. I thought about updating it for this book and adding an unusual flourish or two. In the end, I couldn't think of a single thing I'd want to change about it—and I hope you'll be similarly content.

Preheat the oven to 350°F / 175°C and lightly oil a 9 by 5-inch / 23 by 12cm loaf pan.

In a medium bowl, combine the non-dairy milk and the lemon juice.

In a large bowl, mix the flour, baking soda, baking powder, salt, and cinnamon.

Add the oil, brown sugar, banana, and vanilla to the milk–lemon juice mixture. Whisk to combine. Add these wet ingredients to the dry ingredients and mix until everything is evenly combined and no streaks of dry flour are visible. A few small lumps in the batter are fine. Fold in the walnuts or dark chocolate (if using).

Pour the batter into the loaf pan and bake for 50 to 60 minutes, until the entire loaf is a deep, golden brown and the top is at least slightly domed. (If it's flat, then the bread needs a little extra baking time.) When you check with a toothpick, the toothpick should emerge mostly clean, but a tiny crumb or two is okay. Check the bread at 45 minutes for doneness and continue checking until it's fully baked. If you feel the bread is getting too dark as you bake, you can tent it with foil.

Transfer the loaf to a cooling rack and allow to cool for 20 to 30 minutes. Gently remove the loaf from the pan and allow it to cool to room temperature on the cooling rack before cutting into slices. The loaf can be stored in an airtight container at room temperature for up to 3 days or frozen for up to 8 weeks.

Acknowledgments

A huge thank-you to Ten Speed Press for supporting my career as an author and encouraging me to grow. Every opportunity to work with Kelly Snowden and Emma Campion is a gift. For this project, it was my pleasure to have Claire Yee as my editor. Claire, thank you for your insight, intelligence, and amazing organization! Gabby Ureña, thank you for ushering this process along thoughtfully and for keeping me on track.

Ashley McLaughlin, "photographer" is such an insufficient word to describe your role in this book and the others we've worked on together. Photographer, yes, but also stylist, creative director, recipe brainstormer, and emotional support system. Thank you for wearing so many hats, always with kindness and generosity.

I'm grateful to Chef Ashlee Redger for her feedback and hard work in bringing my recipes to life for photography. Thanks, too, to culinary assistants Alanna Wolohan and Debbi Thompson. Finally, thank you to my loyal and mighty team of recipe testers for their hard work, attention to detail, and enthusiasm.

Chris-Parris Lamb, I'm so grateful for your wisdom, smarts, reassurance, and encouragement, not to mention nearly twenty years of friendship.

The premise for this book is inspired by work from Alicia Silverstone, fellow macro bowl enthusiast Kim-Julie Hansen, everyone who was ever a part of Angelica Kitchen, Joy Pierson and Bart Potenza of Candle Cafe, Ann Gentry, the authors of *The New Laurel's Kitchen*, and Matthew Frazier.

To all my friends, thanks for cheering me on and occasionally reminding me that I actually do love to cook. Mom, you were the first artist I admired. Everything that I create has in some way been inspired by you.

Finally, I'm so grateful to New York City restaurants and the people who keep them running. I thank them for feeding me in the moments when my own beans, greens, and grains are not enough.

About the Contributors

Gena Hamshaw is a registered dietitian nutritionist, a recipe developer, and the author of *Food52 Vegan* (2017), *Power Plates* (2018), and *The Vegan Week* (2022). She shares vegan recipes on her blog, *The Full Helping,* which she has written since 2009. Gena lives in New York City, where she can frequently be found scouting out the best vegan pomodoro pastas and marinara pizza pies in town.

Ashley McLaughlin is a food photographer and stylist who specializes in capturing the artistry and essence of culinary creations for her dynamic group of clients. With a keen eye for detail and a love for aesthetics, she aims to evoke an appreciation for the craftsmanship and creativity behind every recipe. Ashley lives in Fort Collins, Colorado, with her husband, Chris, and daughter, Lennon. Beyond photography, Ashley loves spending time with her family and friends, being active outdoors, and eating croissants whenever possible.

Index

Published in the United States by Ten Speed Press, an imprint of the Crown Publishing Group, a division of Penguin Random House LLC, New York. TenSpeed.com

Ten Speed Press and the Ten Speed Press colophon are registered trademarks of Penguin Random House LLC.

Typeface: Monotype's Tellumo

Library of Congress Cataloging-in-Publication Data is on file with the publisher.
Names: Hamshaw, Gena, author. | McLaughlin, Ashley, photographer.
Title: A grain, a green, a bean: one simple formula, countless meatless meals / Gena Hamshaw of the Full Helping Blog ; photography by Ashley McLaughlin.
Identifiers: LCCN 2024027575 (print) | LCCN 2024027576 (ebook) | ISBN 9781984863201 (hardcover) | ISBN 9781984863218 (ebook)
Subjects: LCSH: Meat substitutes. | Vegan cooking. | LCGFT: Cookbooks.
Classification: LCC TX838 .H36 2025 (print) | LCC TX838 (ebook) | DDC 641.5/6362—dc23/eng/20240907
LC record available at https://lccn.loc.gov/2024027575
LC ebook record available at https://lccn.loc.gov/2024027576

Hardcover ISBN: 978-1-9848-6320-1
eBook ISBN: 978-1-9848-6321-8

Printed in China

Acquiring editor: Kelly Snowden | Project editor: Claire Yee
Production editor: Liana Faughnan
Art director: Emma Campion
Production designers: Mari Gill and Mara Gendell
Production and prepress color manager: Jane Chinn
Copy editor: Carole Berglie | Proofreader: Andrea C. Peabbles
Indexer: Elizabeth Parson
Publicist: Lauren Chung | Marketer: Joey Lozada

10 9 8 7 6 5 4 3 2 1

First Edition